An Arkansas Rhodes Scholar, CLAUD NELSON earned an honors degree in law and a diploma "with distinction" in economics and government at Oxford, taught three years in the South, and in 1926 joined the War Prisoners' Aid of the YMCA, serving in Russia, the United States and Germany. During the Second World War, he was national director of the World Student Service Fund, and later an executive of WPA, serving in New York and later in Italy.

He represented the YMCA's of North America in Italy a total of eighteen years (*in absentia* during the second war), and played an important role in opening the doors there, and in the World's Alliance of YMCA's, to Roman Catholic members and leaders.

In the late 'twenties and 'thirties, during a gap in his Italian service, Claud Nelson served the national student YMCA, and later the Fellowship of Reconciliation, as Southern secretary, pioneering in race relations, and writing *Can Guns Settle Strikes?* when three Southern governors called out the troops against textile strikers.

Retired from the YMCA on his return from Italy in 1951, he served the cause of religious liberty on the staff of the National Council of Churches nine years, helping to determine the ecumenical orientation of his department, and writing a booklet on Church and State.

Since 1960 Dr. Nelson has served the National Conference of Christians and Jews as a consultant, edited *Dialogue,* covered the preparations for and all four sessions of the Second Vatican Council for Religious News Service, and wrote *The Second Vatican Council and All Christians*, published as the Council opened.

Religion and Society
The Ecumenical Impact

Religion and Society
The Ecumenical Impact

by CLAUD D. NELSON

WITH A PREFACE BY *Lewis Webster Jones*

SHEED AND WARD: NEW YORK

© *Sheed and Ward, Inc., 1966*

Library of Congress Catalog Card Number: 66-22020

Manufactured in the United States of America

AUTHOR'S FOREWORD

"Religion and Society" is too vast a subject for one who is neither theologian nor sociologist. A lifetime of involvement in one phase or another of the ecumenical movement suggested the limiting phrase, "The Ecumenical Impact."

The next limitation was the narrowing from a philosophical-historical consideration to an experiential-reportorial approach—encouraged by five years of reporting the Second Vatican Council, in both preparation and process.

This approach accounts for a large element of personal opinion from which the author has tried to screen out mere prejudice. It has seemed to him also to dispense him from the necessity of writing concerning every item that the title might suggest. For example, volumes are being written, appropriately, on the rapid urbanization of society in the United States and the consequent challenge to religion. Chapters three to eight treat of fields in which the author has been professionally active for many years. Although urbanization affects and is affected by developments in each of those areas, the author has acquired a first-hand familiarity and feeling for them which he cannot claim with regard to urban problems as such.

The author's hope is to invite attention to a potent and relatively new sociological factor—not to propose solutions or conclusions. His experience in writing these chapters has been that they persist in becoming more open-ended as to conclusions but more secure in direction, savoring less of debate than of dialogue.

The writing of this book was made possible only through the generosity of my employers, the venturesome encouragement of an ecumenically mature publisher, and the unfailing devotion and support of my wife.

CLAUD D. NELSON

PREFACE

I have had the privilege of being associated with Dr. Claud D. Nelson for the last five years. During my presidency of the National Conference of Christians and Jews we were colleagues on a project dealing with Religious Freedom and Public Affairs, which has been an important enterprise of the NCCJ. It has brought together able and informed people of diverse backgrounds to confront the many problems of church-state relations in a free, pluralistic society; among them such matters as religious observances in the public schools, public support for parochial schools, birth control and the law. The Conference sponsored dialogues between members of the clergy throughout the country dealing with inter-religious relationships and conflicts, as these affected American communities.

Dr. Nelson's book is not, however, a report on this NCCJ project. Nor does Dr. Nelson speak for the Conference. His book is his contribution to the continuing dialogue among many thoughtful people which this particular project, and indeed the whole program of NCCJ, seeks to encourage and stimulate.

Dr. Nelson does not offer this book to the public as a scholarly analysis of the problems he discusses; it is rather a recording of his personal attitudes and beliefs, developed over many decades of reflective experience.

His experience has not been of the ivory tower variety. He took part in the work of the Y.M.C.A. in prisoner-of-war camps in Europe and America in both world wars. Textile strikers passed him through their lines to interview an employer for his pamphlet, "Can Guns Settle Strikes?"; later, Congressman Maury Maverick called him to testify before a House committee investigating the use of troops to put down the five-state textile strike of 1934. He organized and led a non-segregated Institute on International Relations in Atlanta over the opposition of the American Legion in the mid-'thirties. Although he has not been afraid of controversy, his aim and role have always been those of the reconciler.

It is not accidental, therefore, that he was drawn to the ecumenical movement, and has been active in it for many years. He had an indispensable role in opening the Italian Y.M.C.A. in 1945 to Roman Catholics: members, boards and staff. This, in turn, greatly facilitated the adoption of an ecumenical policy by the World's Alliance of Young Men's Christian Associations in 1950.

This is an important book. Dr. Nelson's long and varied experience, and his personal insight, qualify him to comment with wisdom on the relationship of God and man in the complex society of the second half of the twentieth century.

LEWIS WEBSTER JONES
Chairman of the Board
and Chief Executive Officer
Joint Council on Economic Education

CONTENTS

CONTENTS

Religion and Society
The Ecumenical Impact

1

RELIGION
AND THE FREE SOCIETY
An Historical Introduction

Bishop Emilianos, representative of Ecumenical Patriarch Athenagoras at the Vatican Council, speaking under the auspices of the Saint Paul Foundation on the ecumenical necessity of religious liberty in Rome, on November 25, 1965, observed that the vertical and horizontal relationships of man, i.e., the theological and the sociological, must be coordinated. That task is not undertaken in this book. But the book is written and is offered to the reader in the consciousness that that coordination has been too long deferred. The churches, and their theologians, are beginning to wake up: witness the "social Christianity" of the last several decades among North American and European Protestants and the pronounced and pervasive pastoral emphasis of the Second Vatican Council. When this awakening shall have reached the point of ecumenical coordination, there is hope that sociologists will more generally consider not only the importance but the positive values of man's vertical relations.

Religions have influenced social development throughout history, sometimes directly, sometimes indirectly, sometimes for worse, sometimes for better—certainly not always on the side of freedom. We shall in this book assume that if we are to see a "great society" in America, it must be a free society. Our general purpose, therefore, is to examine some aspects or elements of our society which today are not free, and even in some cases obstruct

3

freedom, and see whether, and how, religious forces can be brought to bear in such a way as to move America toward a freer society.

We shall have to listen to those who say that religion today, organized religion at any rate, is not capable of influencing society, and to those who say that social problems are not a proper concern of religion. We must take account of the immense forces of the Left dictatorships that do not include freedom, in a sense that Americans can accept, as a characteristic of the ideal society: to them, both religion and freedom are opium for the people. This has been true also of the Fascist-Nazi movement and of the extreme Right today. Unlike the communist leaders, those of the far Right are ready to administer the opium; they fight a larger freedom in the name of a narrow one, an ecumenical and ethical religion on the basis of a religion that is circumscribed and antisocial.

In the American setting, we shall have in mind theistic religion within the Judeo-Christian tradition—without prejudice and usually without relevance to Islam, Buddhism, or the surviving religions of American Indians. As distinguishing—or at least identifying—traits of this religious tradition, it is sufficient at this point to mention two or three that are relevant to our purpose. Unlike the gods of Olympus, its deity is ethical and dependable—and One, not a legion. He is not the detached, impassive, and unapproachable entity predicated in Deism: He is concerned. He hears the cry of the poor, the oppressed, the penitent. He is the God of the Ten Commandments and of the Sermon on the Mount. Thus every one of His created children is of supreme worth. To offend one of them is to offend their Father. And all these children are one family; to offend *one* of them—by any injustice or indignity—is to offend all of them: a crime against humanity. Not only are these beliefs—this faith—normative for churches and synagogues; they are intellectually and morally binding on all believers.

It can scarcely be doubted that if all organizations and individuals who honor the Judeo-Christian heritage conformed their actions to their words, the effect on society would be wide and deep.

Today, however, many would maintain that all of this heritage that is still sociologically relevant is included in secular humanism. Insofar as this is true, believers may rejoice, and cooperate thankfully with their fellow humanists. They need not insist in proprietary and condescending fashion on the debt which they think is owed by the secular humanism of the West to the Jewish and Christian faiths. Repentant, rather, for religious wars and inquisitorial persecutions, ancient and modern, they must continue to press forward toward the mark of their own high calling; the claims of faith will be well served by living examples of its relevance. If believers are bent on converting secular humanists to religious faith, the first requirement is not to fall behind them in redemptive service to society. This author, accordingly, while convinced of the net value of organized religion, is here much less concerned with its vindication than with the challenge to all believers to show their faith by their works.

We are not assuming that the function of religion is to support the accepted values of society. It has created and must continue to discover and formulate values. It must judge, evaluate and, if necessary, help to revise accepted values. Society automatically judges religion, but on a contemporary and perhaps ephemeral basis. Although religion witnesses ineffectually to eternal truth, the truth sits in constant, imperishable judgment on society.

The roots of religion cannot be something negative—anathemas, prohibitions, penalties—a defensive stance toward the world that God loves, whose redemption religion seeks. God is indeed He whose judgments are true and righteous altogether; all must stand in awe of them. But if ever men were frightened into righteousness, modern men are not likely to be, and are less and less likely to be frightened into abstaining from evil. They are more likely to respond to Pope John the pastor than to Torquemada the Grand Inquisitor; to Quakers preaching love than to revivalists preaching hell-fire.

Another caveat, and we quote Dr. Franklin Littell (*Christian Advocate,* October 21, 1965): "A True Church will be a blessing to any people—but that is not its reason for existence. A person who argues that religion is of benefit to a society knows only third-person religion. First-person religion is faithfulness regardless of consequences—(thus a threat to the idolatrous society or state but a blessing to the open society)."

In another chapter we shall look further at the role of religion in our society. Let us now catalog briefly some problems upon whose solution progress toward a freer society depends, and to whose solution religious men and women should and probably must contribute. Sometimes religion will attempt to influence society through government; sometimes through education; always through the action of its convinced adherents.

Among the most pressing challenges, worldwide in scope and urgent for the United States, are the achieving and maintaining of peace with justice; the elimination of discrimination based on color, creed, class or national origin; reaching and preserving a tolerable ratio between population and available food supply; raising the earning capacity and opportunity of the vast majority of the world's population, now existing below the level of decent self-support. These problems are inextricably bound together. We shall not achieve a just and durable peace with over half of the human race victimized by poverty, ignorance, oppression, color bars, lack of equal opportunity. The problems of poverty and of population are not separable. Since both are at present vaster and more acute among black, brown and yellow peoples than among those of lighter pigmentation, white men will either hasten to share their material and technical capital with others or be subjected to a pitiless and vengeful revolution. Whites may in the second alternative delude themselves into thinking that they are defending civilization when in fact they will be sacrificing it to a spurious and selfish doctrine of racial superiority propagated by Madison Grant, Lothrop Stoddard, Adolf Hitler and his minions, white citizens' councils, and—may Heaven help us—by professing Christians who misquote Scripture as though God, not Noah, had cursed Ham, and invent an anthropology that makes all Negroes Ham's descendants.

No less absurd, and more widely incriminating and weakening of religious forces, are anti-Semitism and the mutual suspicion and hostility between Protestants and Roman Catholics.[1] It was the virulent anti-Catholic propaganda against Alfred E. Smith in the national election campaign of 1928 that led to the founding of the National Conference of Christians and Jews (NCCJ). Eight quadrenniums later (thanks in no small part to the work of NCCJ) voters were able to distinguish between their religious and political loyalties and prejudices sufficiently to make possible the election of a Catholic—a Catholic who, in turn, could be loyal to the faith of his church without looking to it for political directives.

Relations between Protestants and Catholics are definitely improving. This is part of the ecumenical movement—of which more later. There is room and need for the still embryonic fellowship to permeate congregations and communities, but surely we shall not return to the depths of the earlier Protestant nativism: we now know both the necessity and the efficacy of vigilance. Much of what Protestants are convinced that they must continue to combat in certain Catholic positions—and vice-versa—will be considered in our study of church-state relations.

Anti-Semitism is much more deeply embedded in our traditions and mores than Protestant-Catholic tensions. To decrease the latter will facilitate the extirpation of those prejudices that have been created by false Christian teaching—now already being corrected or outlawed by both Protestant-Orthodox and Catholic world bodies. Part of the remedy lies in the very fact of Jewish participation, by right and as equals—as, for example, in the NCCJ and its dialogue groups. But textbooks must be corrected. Long-standing habits of thought, speech and action must be corrected. Jews and Christians must get to know each other in a religious frame of

---

[1] Henceforth, "Roman" will be omitted unless required for clear identification. "Roman" is a proper part of the name of the Catholic Church with headquarters in Rome. But there are Greek Catholics, Anglo-Catholics, and so forth. Protestants regularly recite a creed expressing belief in "the holy catholic church."

reference—a matter of the greatest difficulty. Jews and Gentiles must become acquainted on a deeper human level than the market place. There is much unfinished business for NCCJ, Newman Clubs, Student Christian Associations, Jewish lay organizations— for churches and synagogues, for the world.

RELATIONS BETWEEN RELIGION AND GOVERNMENT

Society has committed many problems and delegated many tasks to government: local, provincial, national, international. Religion must therefore have proper relations with government if, at many points, it is to have mutually profitable relations with society. Conversely, relations between government and religion are largely conditioned by the nature of the given society and the place of religion in it. One desirable, ideally necessary relation between religion and the state is described as religious liberty. Its importance for religion and for freedom justifies extended consideration later in this essay. Part of the problem here, and in areas that we are about to mention, is that religious bodies do not agree among themselves; i.e., interreligious tensions complicate relations between churches and governments and between religion and society.

This is notably the case with regard to education. It was long the monopoly of the church, both theoretically and practically, when priests and monks were the only literate members of the community—and scarcely less so in Puritan New England and many frontier communities. Today Protestants are divided among themselves as to the role and the character of religious instruction and practices in the public school curriculum and buildings. Catholics—and Jews—are perhaps less divided among themselves. But this does not greatly facilitate—if at all—the formation of two blocs, one uniting "liberals," the other, "conservatives." The frame of reference of such a hypothetical classification varies from one faith group to another. One example: Missouri Synod Lutherans and Catholics both operate parochial schools. In each case they may be divided among themselves as to the need of federal aid to public schools. But many Catholics tend to feel that they would be victims of gross and glaring injustice if federal aid for elementary and secondary public schools were not extended to include parochial schools (though we have not heard too much of this argument with regard to local and state tax support). Lutherans, on the contrary, tend to feel that tax support for church-related schools would confuse the roles and compromise the character of church and state, contrary to the wise provisions of the First Amendment. It would also, in their view, adulterate the voluntary character of the parochial school—an element that is essential for its religious task. They would see injustice and violation of conscience in being forced to support instruction in a faith which they could not accept. Orthodox Jews would welcome tax support for their schools. Many, of all faiths and of no faith, would fear the consequences if any tax stimulus were offered for the creation of numerous and heterogeneous—religious or religious-labeled—private schools. In the resultant rivalry and confusion, education has been sadly undernourished.

Similar tensions exist with regard to bus transportation to private schools and to Bible reading, prayer, and religious instruction, practices and observances in public schools. Many conservative Protestants join with most Jews and with the National Council of Churches (NCCC) in opposing tax grants for religiously-affiliated schools, but favor prayer and Bible reading in public schools, which the NCCC and the Jews oppose. Tensions are found also in the matter of tax exemptions on a religious basis, the closing of business on Saturday (the Sabbath for Jews, Adventists and other Sabbatarians), the dispensing of contraceptive advice or devices, the military chaplaincy and the general relation between law and morality. To some of these items we must return. For the moment, it is enough to point out that religious forces are spending much of their energy in frustrating each other, with less than maximum edification of their opposite numbers and potential allies, and often impeding religion from exerting its proper and possible role in society. Here indeed is a vast and vital area that cries out for the honest speaking and earnest listening that we call dialogue—the topic of a later section. Before we look briefly at the large-scale dialogue which is the ecumenical movement, let us review in outline the varying forms assumed by church-state relations in Europe and America during the centuries since Constantine.

THROUGH ESTABLISHMENT TO PLURALISM

A study of great interest and relevance to our topic would be a comparison of the direction and force of the impact of Christians on society before and after Constantine. But the topic is wider than the author's competence, or the projected scope of this book. Without pursuing the comparison, however, we may raise two or three questions whose consideration should stimulate further thought and stirring of conscience with regard to establishment, or any attempt by religion to wield temporal power. Accepting the legend of Constantine's vision, "In this sign" (the Cross) "you shall conquer," we must ask whether he did not transform the symbol from one of loving sacrifice to one of conquest, which continued to distort the Christian witness at least through the Crusades. Did his policy not to a large degree seduce the Christian community into accepting the "Kingdoms of the world and the glory of them" (Matthew iv, 8–10, RSV), the third of Satan's offers that Jesus had rejected? What, apart from the security of the state's protection and the enjoyment of the state's power, robbed Christians of a fervor and a momentum that was turning the world upside down? These are not just rhetorical questions. The memory of a crucified and resurrected leader became less fresh and direct as the generations passed. The expectation of his immediate and triumphant return was becoming faint. Even if we should conclude that Constantine's establishment was a calamity, who can be sure that we would have been wiser or truer to the faith than those who accepted it?

Seven centuries after Constantine, both church and empire settled into a division between East and West, succumbing in large measure to the same cultural, ethnic and political rivalries. How truly and effectively East and West had been united in the intervening centuries is a large question. But the transfer of imperial power to Constantinople, and the subsequent division of the empire, might not have been accompanied by the formal schism in the church, or the breach might have been repaired sooner, had imperial and ecclesiastical power not been so closely intermeshed—and in many ways so similar.

Meanwhile, in western Europe, a unity of purpose and an accommodation of authority had related church and state to each other in ways that, at least in the nostalgic memory of some Catholic spokesmen, seem almost idyllic. In spite of troublesome heresies (and scarcely less troublesome saints), some intransigent emperors and occasionally overambitious popes, there was a sufficiently close union of church and state to afford many of the blessings of theocracy, with sufficient distinction of authority and function to avoid most of its defects. From the point of view of order and authority, and of uniformity of the faith professed, western Europe for a few centuries after Charlemagne was well-nigh a sacral society. Men could confess their vices and sins, do penance, and have their normal place in society—Gentiles, that is: the nearly sacral society had then no hospitality toward Jews.

But centrifugal forces began to unravel the close-knit fabric. Men discovered that Europe was not the globe, this planet was not the universe, and probably not its center. The growth of commerce, the spread of printed materials, the revival of classical learning, the end of its monopoly by the clergy—all combined with the development of experimental science to produce a ferment. There issued from it almost a new breed of men, self-reliant and inquisitive. They questioned the divine right of kings at Runnymede, and democracy was foreshadowed. With money, borrowed or saved, men could vastly increase their earnings; capitalism was born, and Christians began to doubt that interest was wicked usury.

In and with this medieval-modern transition ferment appeared

nationalism, and a self-determining individualism which contributed to laicism and then secularism, democracy, and the second
great schism in Christendom. While the Reformers were anathema-
tized for centuries as heretics, strictly theological doctrinal differences between Rome and Geneva are being discussed today, and
will increasingly be discussed, as differences between brothers
(e.g., Hans Küng's examination of Karl Barth's doctrine of justification). But a schism there was, and is. Differences as to the
nature of the church and its order are at least partly theological,
and perhaps all the more stubborn for not being as readily submis-
sible to the evidence of Scripture as is the doctrine of justification.

The Reformation schism enjoyed vital political support from the
exponents of the growing nationalism of northern Germany, Scan-
dinavia, England, Holland and Switzerland, and facilitated the establishment of national and provincial churches. These new alli-
ances were in general no better and no worse for society than the
grander alliance which they fractured and partly replaced. The
unity of the West was ruptured, but there was (not necessarily
because of the fracture, but along with it) a new dynamism in both
religion and government—rather more marked among the schis-
matic Nordic peoples than among the Latins and south Germans,
who remained loyal to Rome. But, in a given country, the generally accepted rule was that the official religion of the nation was
accepted by all its citizens: pluralism was below the horizon. If it
was beginning to emerge, it was still labeled schism or heresy.
Church and state had distinguishable functions, but each was
dependent on the other for normal functioning: their gears intermeshed—and sometimes clashed, since each was trying to use, if
not to dominate, the other. At this point, we should begin to look
at the New World.

THE AMERICAN EXPERIENCE

The Pilgrim Fathers came to New England to escape what they
felt to be a tyrannous establishment, and set up one of their own.

If some of them hoped that its rule could be that of God Himself, a theocracy, the form was to become very soon, paradoxically, a free church establishment, which was to survive in Massachusetts until 1833. The free church had freedom for itself: convinced that it embodied the divine will and was bound to enforce it, it saw no place for another church or for other freedom.

Something of the ideas and temper of theocracy was to reappear in the Church of the Latter Day Saints of Jesus Christ. There may be traces of it among Doukhobors, Hutterites and Amish. Some would look askance at the ideas of all these groups. But many a religious worker in our religiously fragmented urban areas would welcome the revival of the sense of a community under one God and one faith—if not a true theocracy, at least some approach to a people religiously united in fellowship and aspiration. Dr. William Cate, in *The Ecumenical Scandal on Main Street* (1965) pleading for an approach to the community as a whole, says that organized (denominational) religion "can be one of the most disintegrative influences in the community."

But the road from a near-theocratic establishment to a diverse community integrated by a shared faith is neither direct, short nor smooth. The search for freedom, the growing and spreading conviction that men must be equal in the view of human laws as they are by divine law, and diverse readings of divine law—all combine to produce a religiously pluralistic society. During the colonial period this development was attended by suffering, and even martyrdom, but resulted in substantial progress toward freedom in Rhode Island, Pennsylvania, Maryland and Virginia.

During the transition period toward federal union, the Congress of the Confederation took a long step toward freedom in the Ordinance for the Government of the Northwest Territory, 1787, which provided:

and for extending the fundamental principle of civil and religious liberty. . . .

Article I. No person, demeaning himself in a peaceable and orderly manner, shall ever be molested on account of his mode of worship, or religious sentiments, in the said territory.

Article III. Religion, morality, and knowledge, being necessary to good government and the happiness of mankind, schools and the means of education shall forever be encouraged. . . .

The Ordinance was confirmed by the Federal Congress in 1789. It has typed our system of government of the territories.

Here is religious liberty, but no indifference, and no absolute wall of separation. In fact, the twenty-ninth section of the public land, in each township, was set aside for impartial aid to religion, and part of the proceeds was used for the benefit of two Protestant-oriented colleges. The practice was discontinued in 1860 in order to avoid discrimination or involvement in sectarian rivalries. (*Church and State* [1953], a pamphlet published for the Department of Religious Liberty, NCCC)

The Confederation Congress had also rejected a proposal by the Papal Nuncio in France that it act to secure the appointment of a non-British prelate for American Catholics in place of their former British superior. Franklin explained privately why this could not be done, but transmitted the proposal to Congress, which answered that, the application "being purely spiritual, it is without the jurisdiction and powers of Congress . . . to permit or refuse it, these powers being reserved to the several states individually."[2]

The decisive step in the development of the American pattern

[2] Roman Catholic Bishop John Carroll of Maryland vigorously opposed being subjected to any such *foreign* prelate.

was the inclusion in the Bill of Rights, First Amendment to the Constitution, 1791, of the provision: "Congress shall make no law respecting an establishment of religion, or prohibiting the free exercise thereof. . . ." This principle is expressed in all the state constitutions, and might be applied to them, if necessary, through the Supreme Court's interpretation of the post-Civil War Fourteenth Amendment. The doctrine of church-state separation embodied in the Bill of Rights is a perennial subject of interpretation by publicists and by religious bodies. In recent decades the Supreme Court has dealt frequently with it, in cases relating to religion and education. It is not easy to determine when a statute—or a given practice—tends too far toward "an establishment of religion"; nor is it easy to encourage religion, or to recognize with Justice Douglas that "we are a religious people," without laying the foundation for establishment; or to hold the line for "free exercise" without encouraging those who would establish religion —or nonreligion. Some relevant Supreme Court decisions (noted later), the Declaration of Independence, and indeed our entire history, make it clear that our secular state looks upon religion with a benevolent eye.

Father John Courtney Murray, S.J., in *Theological Studies,* June 1953, documented fully a clear distinction between the American doctrine, springing from the concept of a limited state in a society that does not deny the fundamental place of religion, and the European doctrine, constantly combated by Pope Leo XIII, of the self-sufficient state, a heresy that began with the spurious theory of the divine right of kings, was combated by Cardinal Bellarmine, but has returned to haunt this century as totalitarianism.

A religiously pluralistic society, federally speaking, made necessities of church-state separation and religious liberty. These in turn have enabled us to live with pluralism, which has been advantageous for religious minorities but has been one of the factors in the progressive fragmentation (and weakening?) of Protestantism. It is largely true that the good old days never were. In the Protestant heyday, it was not so much a case of a united Protestant leadership as of a general acquiescence of the citizenship in a Protestant-oriented culture.

But Protestant denominations prior to 1850 were not strong on the social gospel. Their revivalists—and later, their institutions—were following the westward march—contributing, it is true, to law and order, but preaching an individual redemption, and adding to their membership. In that period, and still today, membership could involve a minimum of commitment to the church, or to its ideals. Loyalty to the denomination is likely, almost certain, to mean great emphasis on what divides from other denominations, less emphasis on what unites them—which, theoretically taken for granted, is all too likely to be gradually forgotten.

As to the revivalists and the minimum commitment, Dr. Franklin H. Littell has this to say, after noting that church affiliation rose in a hundred years from seven percent to seventy percent of the population:

At the end of this period of mass evangelism, the churches are no longer an embattled minority struggling against unbelief and what our fathers called "infidelism." The problem of the Protestant churches in 1964 is not "infidelism" outside the churches: it is unfaithfulness within.

Here we come to the nub of the matter. For, as much as we have to be thankful for in the mass accessions of membership, attendance and support, the fact is that they were accompanied by a downgrading of membership standards almost to the vanishing point. About the turn of the century, Baptists and Disciples and Methodists—the great revival churches—ended church discipline and virtually wiped out membership requirements. It was the 1908 General Conference of the Methodist Episcopal Church which ended that characteristic Wesleyan practice, probationary membership, for the sake of statistical success.

Again and again, in the blasphemy of the racists, in the wickedness of mobs, in the impudent lying of the Protestant underworld, we live with the price the church must pay for being a purveyor of what Bonhoeffer called "cheap grace." (University of Kansas Law and Society Institute, September 1964)

The affiliate's commitment, along with any feeling of obligation to make an ethical commitment, is also weakened by the current tendency, noted and publicized by Professor Will Herberg: to use the religious label merely for identification, almost without additional implications. This is seen in the armed forces, and in many governmental and other listings. In some cases, perhaps many, persons prefer an identification that does not reveal the racial or national ancestry. Eastern Orthodox have pressed, successfully in a few states, for laws listing them as a recognized fourth faith group. With the addition of Buddhists in Hawaii, and of considerable numbers and two or three varieties of the worshippers of Allah, there may come changes in the present attractiveness of this surface identification, especially for members of the armed forces.

Commitment tends to become even shallower under the impact of an "American" religion—which is mere religiosity. Two quite different forces seek the blessing and support of government: one is primarily religious; the other is primarily political. There are two different kinds of religious pressure in this direction. One sincere and dedicated Protestant denomination has pressed Congress during two decades for a "Christian Amendment" to the Constitution. Sponsors for their cause are available, but the proposal has remained in committee, though hearings have been held. The proponents of this measure have had their pleading recorded in debates, widely broadcast by local stations. The National Council of Churches in 1959 issued a pronouncement opposing an amendment of that character. It was held that the proposed amendment would lead to confusion of the functions of the church with those of the state; that similar attempts, historically, had resulted in violations of liberty, particularly religious liberty; that it would lay a basis for financial discrimination against non-Christians; that it was anti-ecumenical in tendency; and that it would invite pretense and hypocrisy. The other sort of religious pressure is more complex, consisting now of efforts to have the government as an ally—actual if undeclared—of Protestantism, of having it give support to religion in less limited terms. We shall return to this kind of pressure when we come to such questions as religious observances and exercises in the public schools, the Supreme Court decisions beginning with the Champaign case and the proposed Becker Amendment of the 1963–64 Congress.

Politicians (including honest ones) find it advantageous to enlist religious sentiment—specific if that of the majority, general if that proves more serviceable—on their side. Conversely, to offend or alienate it is almost certain to be disadvantageous. The same applies to political parties, and to government as a whole. While this situation may be an evidence that religion is politically influential, it tends to identify it with patriotism, or even with the policy of the moment, especially in the case of international and ideological conflict. Genuine religious faith reinforces patriotism (as it does family loyalty and affection), but it also purifies and transcends it. Neither Jew nor Christian can accept the religiosity that seeks to replace his faith with Americanism.

THE ECUMENICAL MOVEMENT

The twentieth century has witnessed a reversal of the centrifugal movement in Protestantism, or at least an impressive beginning of an opposite motion. There were significant beginnings of cooperation across denominational lines in the nineteenth century. The Young Men's and Young Women's Christian Associations, beginning with a dozen young men in London in 1844, drawn from several denominations, had become international, and strong enough to render valuable service to society, in both Protestant and non-Christian areas before the outbreak of war in 1914. Some of their student counterparts were independent; some were affiliated with the "Y's"; together, they comprised the World's Student

Christian Federation. Associations and Federation had accumulated experience and developed leadership among lay men and women both West and East which were to be of the greatest value in the area of the Protestant churches' foreign missionary activities, and in the movement toward Christian cooperation and unity.

We have noted how much energy has been expended, in predominantly Protestant areas, in denominational rivalry or needless duplication. In seeking to extend the Christian witness and influence among non-Christian peoples, missionaries frequently found that their denominational labels were a source of confusion, and their disunity was a denial of the message they proclaimed. The confusion and the denial were heightened when Catholics and Protestants were active in the same areas; their outer differences, in dress and in the forms of worship, struck the eye, and their theological differences were even more puzzling than the variations in the Protestant confessions. These difficulties confronted the Protestant leaders assembled in the International Missionary Conference in Edinburgh in 1910, which in large and significant measure marks the beginning of the ecumenical movement among Protestants. It gave rise to the International Missionary Council (which in 1961 merged with the World Council of Churches). It also pricked the conscience and stirred the imagination of Protestant leaders and very soon also of Eastern Orthodox, so that there were soon founded the movement for cooperation in "Life and Work" and the movement for exploring the differences in "Faith and Order." The two movements were integrated in the process of formation of the World Council of Churches, officially constituted in Amsterdam in 1948. The influence of the 1910 Edinburgh missionary conference has not been limited to the "separated brethren." The author, steeped in that tradition, returning to Rome in 1961 to study preparations for the Second Vatican Council, was rejoiced to find that one of the outstanding younger leaders of the Catholic efforts in promoting Christian unity had also found challenge and inspiration in the Edinburgh meeting.

The Protestant-Orthodox movement was first ignored by the Vatican and then, as late as 1928, denounced. This does not mean that Catholics had no thirst for the renewal of Christian unity, or were insensitive to the handicap of disunity on the mission field or in relation to the problems of society. Pope John's appeal for Catholic renewal—which would also serve to facilitate Christian reunion—was thus not a cry in the wilderness. Thanks to the work of his Secretariat for Promoting Christian Unity, and of the Council's decree on Ecumenism, Catholics (consulted in advance) responded quickly and affirmatively to the January 1965 proposal of the World Council of Churches to set up a commission of Catholics, Orthodox and Protestants to consider together areas of possible cooperation and joint study of differences and make recommendations to the parent bodies.

Of possibly greater potential than the world conciliar movement, and certainly necessary to its maximum usefulness, is the local and national development of councils of churches. In the United States, the Federal Council of Churches, organized in 1908, merged with other interdenominational agencies in 1950 to create the National Council of the Churches of Christ in the U.S.A. The three other major merging bodies were the Home and Foreign Missions Conferences and the International Council of Religious Education, whose roots included the Sunday-School Associations of the nineteenth century. State and local Councils of Churches are independent of each other and of the national organization.

It should be evident to all that it is easier for Catholics, for Orthodox, and for Jews to have mutually helpful relations with Councils, even though they are more on the order of clearing houses than federations, than with national denominations. Orthodox Churches are now members of the Councils, from local to world level. Recently, one or two Catholic parishes have joined city Councils of Churches, and the diocese of New Mexico has joined the state Council. In March 1965 the President of the National Council of Churches indicated publicly that the Roman Catholic Church is eligible for membership in the NCCC. It is probable that Catholics and Council will prefer to develop relations considerably further at local and state level before beginning serious negotiations nationally.

Meanwhile, one must note that the conciliar movement does not enjoy the participation, world or national, of a number of eligible Protestant bodies: Baptists (over ten million of whom send delegates to the Southern Baptist Convention), Missouri Synod Lutherans, Seventh Day Adventists, and those joining in the National Association of Evangelicals. There is cooperation, both official and unofficial, between some of their units and units of the NCCC. During the past seven years most of these groups have participated in a series of unofficial conversations among leaders of denominations, some inside and some outside the National Council of Churches, without officers, minutes or resolutions, but with encouraging results in mutual understanding and trust.

When one sees how little influence on society can be honestly and indisputably claimed for religion, and reflects on the time and energy misdirected because of the lack of unity and united effort on the part of the Christians, one looks with hope on the development of the ecumenical movement at every level. There is already encouraging evidence that it is adding, and will continue to add, to the religious impact on society.

The most noteworthy improvements so far are in the areas of Christian-Jewish, Protestant-Catholic and Negro-white relationships. Some initial and tentative steps have been taken in a struggle, not yet fully ecumenical, against poverty and war.

The heaviest responsibility rests upon Christians for the influence of religion in society, because of their numbers, their wealth, their relation to the power structures, and their acceptance, always implicit and progressively more explicit, of responsibility for the dignity and wholeness of every human being. In the United States, Christians must clear the way for increased understanding and cooperation with Jews, combating anti-Semitism and joining them, on both sociological and theological grounds, in removing every form of injustice and discrimination from our communities.

2

RELIGIOUS RESPONSIBILITY
IN THE SOCIAL ORDER

Before considering religion's responsibility in society, we should note some evidences of its influence, negative, mixed, or positive. Religious people must look at the negative, for they have the heavy responsibility to counteract it, and eliminate it. If one looks at such things as the Crusades and the Inquisition, directed both against Jewish "infidels" and against heretics, and the religious wars, the one against the Cathari or Albigensians and those of the post-Reformation period, he realizes how much evil can be done in the name of religion, and even with relatively pure intentions and good conscience.

A mixed picture is that of the relation between religious forces and slavery, racism, war, and religious liberty; many religious men and women have battled for the right, but the churches have been too often complacent. Mixed also have been the results of Christian missions to non-European countries, where along with schools, hospitals and the proclamation of high ethical standards went the promotion, not always intended, of Western culture and economic and political interests, and, too often, a frustrating and esoteric sectarianism.

But even those who maintain that religion is a private concern having no right to meddle with political, economic or other social matters will find it hard to overlook the indirect effects of religion even when the believer considers it only a private matter. Does the changing, the "conversion," of an individual from one who is disoriented, perhaps dissipated, and indifferent or hostile to society, into one who is answering the appeal of religion, causing him to face about and become an upright man, have no significance for society? It is not easy to ignore one's own observations of such examples, nor the empirical and theoretical testimony to the genuineness and effectiveness of conversions. Such testimony is found, for example, in Harold Begbie's *Twice-Born Men,* with examples that can be multiplied from the records of the Salvation Army, and in William James' *Varieties of Religious Experience.* John Wesley did not preach primarily to or about society, but there is abundant testimony that the thousands in England who changed their attitude and their conduct as a result of his preaching exerted a powerful influence on the society of that day. The historian Lecky observed that the preaching of Wesley and his companions helped to save England from having its counterpart of the French Revolution.

As Americans occupied territories to the west in the first century of our independence, it can scarcely be doubted that the net influence of preachers and pastors, Protestant and Catholic, was on the side of good citizenship. When religion helps to strengthen family ties, truth-telling, honesty in business, it is not merely a private matter.

Christians and Jews have long pioneered and maintained hospitals and schools. Their ministry to victims of war was well under way even in the nineteenth century. In the twentieth it has not only expanded on their initiative to include chaplaincy to the armed forces and welfare service in hospitals, but now embraces helpful service to millions of refugees and, during both world wars, included a remarkable ministry to prisoners of war.

A recent poll indicated that those who consider that the influence of religion in the United States is increasing were far fewer in 1964 than seven years earlier, when two-thirds of those polled were of the opinion that religion's influence was increasing. In 1964, according to a Gallup survey, only one-third of those polled held to that opinion. But even totalitarian governments find it hard to deal with religion. One recalls that Mussolini said that a nation must have a religion. The Communist Party, theoretically atheist, makes or inspires intermittent efforts to abolish religion. In Russia, where Christianity in the days of the Tsars was fostered by the Eastern Orthodox Church as primarily and almost exclusively matters of worship and of private morality, and was closely identified with the state, it is perhaps paradoxical that religion is proving very tenacious in spite of the Party's efforts to wipe it out. This is partly because of the very fact that worship was and is central in Orthodoxy, and church institutions are relatively less important.

In the United States our government, our state papers and Supreme Court decisions, and our society in general, treat religion at least as an ongoing factor in our national life, an entity whose existence and right to exist are not in question and which is sometimes advantageous to society. Currently, for example, religious forces community by community are being invited by the government to take part in the war on poverty. Here it is important to note what may be a very significant change that is taking place in the attitude of the churches toward antisocial forces. Much of the church's ministry that we note in this chapter is really salvage work. Now the executive of the Commission of the National Council of Churches on the Church and Economic Life, Dr. Cameron P. Hall, observes that while former generations of Christians have sought the "mitigation of poverty," the current generation "will not rest until it is eliminated." While one may reflect that on this basis it will be a long time before believers may rest "at ease in Zion," one must add that resting at ease was not the challenge of the prophets. When churches and synagogues unite for the duration in the war on poverty, and in the concomitant wars against racial injustice and war itself, we shall have a genuine and a promising test of the influence of religion in society. The test might well prove negative, unless the churches value human welfare above their religious institutions. The great test is whether one is willing to sacrifice himself. But while this may lead individuals to martyrdom, willingness to sacrifice its institutions might redeem a church.

LIMITED RESPONSIBILITY

As we shift the focus of our attention from religion's influence to its responsibility with regard to society, we need to note that "responsibility" is meaningful primarily for organized religion. All religion may in one way or another *influence* society, in whole or in part. But it is difficult to see how we can assume a *responsibility* in any meaningful social sense where there is no channel for its corporate discharge. We must not forget, however, that whatever responsibility for or in society is properly assignable to organized religion, the discharge of that responsibility may quite properly be effected through individuals—chiefly lay but not excluding clerical —motivated, even inspired, and to some extent guided, by religious organizations.

The trend in the United States, and in world Christian bodies, seems to be rather steadily toward the assertion, or at least the acceptance, by organized religious bodies of varying degrees of responsibility for what happens in the social order. One of the recent manifestations of this trend was in the position taken in the spring of 1965 by leaders of the National Association of Evangelicals; noting that social concern among evangelicals is quite strong, they said that "a theology for such a concern needs joint development." (*Religious News Service,* May 27, 1965)

One of the major emphases in the Second Vatican Council was that on the pastoral attitude of the Roman Catholic Church in and toward the world as a secular society. This is attested both by the pre-Council exhortations of Pope John XXIII and the promulgation of the "Constitution on the Church in the Modern World." That the same is true of the National Council of Churches is attested by the very names of its departments (e.g., church and society, race relations, education, religious liberty, international affairs, family life), by its occasional pronouncements, and by the volume of conservative criticism directed against it because of its involvement in social controversy. The World Council of Churches is firmly committed and constantly active in social concerns such as religious liberty, better race relations, opposition to anti-Semitism, international justice and peace.

This trend does not mean necessarily responsibility *for* the social order. Indeed, the late Father Gustave Weigel, S.J., Professor of Ecclesiology at Woodstock College, observed: "What happens in the secular society cannot be the responsibility of the church unless by mutual contract this phase of secular life has been committed to the church by the secular society itself." This negation stems from a sharp distinction between the ecclesiastical and secular orders, a distinction much sharper than their actual separation. Perhaps this hypothetical contract was an implicit assumption in Western Christianity before the Reformation and the rise of national governments; reference to it seems almost to carry a slight nostalgic note. Father Weigel, however, was thoroughly pragmatic in saying that he did not think that the hypothetical contract was real anywhere in the world today. He went on to say, "I must also assume that the church has a *preoccupation* with the social order of the secular world. It cannot be indifferent to it . . . sacral and secular authority, however, live in one and the same world; one and the same man, both sacral and secular, simultaneously under the directives of church and secular society." The church, he said, "in just being a church helps secular society by way of by-product." He saw in selfishness, individual and collective, the fatal enemy of any social order. It was his opinion that while unselfishness can exist in men who are not consciously religious, such men are few. In general he aligned himself with the view that you cannot get the fruits of religion without its roots. Hence secular powers should foster the work of the church, which contributes to the well-being of the secular social order. This was not just a plea for his church:

All religions—which in this address I call the church—teach ascetical self-control, at least to the degree of effective submission to just law even when the law is purely secular. All religions believe in the virtues of equity, sobriety and honesty. All religions somehow have a vision of the universal fellowship of men. These virtues contribute immensely to a beneficent secular social order. Where these virtues thrive the secular social order is healthy and dynamic. Police power cannot produce these virtues, but the church can inculcate them better than any other agency. (Washington Institute of NCCJ's Project, Religious Freedom and Public Affairs 1962)

On the same occasion Dr. Jaroslav Pelikan, a Lutheran now of Yale Divinity School, expressed dismay at the minimal commitment of many Protestants, so slight that they could not really be called Christian. While they assert their allegiance to biblical morality, and would probably cite the Ten Commandments or the Sermon on the Mount in defining the ethical life, their allegiance is general and sentimental and does not find expression in the social crises of our day. Their private morality is due more to the age-long customs of their community of faith than to personal conviction. Thus implying or taking for granted religion's social responsibility, he despaired of its achieving significant results without theological orientation and driving force.

To strengthen any program for the discharge of the Christian's responsibility in the social order, one would have to develop the churches' understanding that the "people of God" are mainly lay men and women, the expression of whose faith is not confined to church attendance and activities on behalf of the religious institution, but who are motivated and trained to express their faith in the family, in their vocations, and in the community. In order to bring this about, laymen must also take initiative, even accepting the risk of being accused of anticlericalism. There are many indications today of commitment on the part of the churches, Catholic,

Orthodox and Protestant, to develop a program in which clergy and laity find their proper places for maintaining the direct prophetic witness of religion and its indirect expression in the social order. The Second Vatican Council encouraged and potentially enlarged the responsible participation of lay men and women by receiving some as auditors and consultants, by a strong fundamental statement in the Constitution on the Church, by a more detailed consideration in the Decree on the Apostolate of the Laity, and—perhaps most of all—by promulgating the Constitution on the Church in the Modern World. The Orthodox have long had lay theologians, and deplore any discounting of lay responsibility or status. The Federal Council of Churches once had a layman as president; its successor, the National Council of Churches, has a layman as its chief executive officer.

If the Incarnation is accepted by Christians not only in the sense that God was uniquely present in the person and ministry of Jesus of Nazareth, but also in the sense that He is constantly seeking to express Himself in all the affairs and all the inhabitants of the "world" which He "loved," it seems as if Christians should have an irresistible imperative for surrendering themselves in positive fashion to the discharge of the responsibility in society.

Rabbi Emil L. Fackenheim, Professor of Philosophy at the University of Toronto, likewise a speaker at the NCCJ's 1962 Washington Institute, protested vigorously against divorcing the religious and social realms: "It was the distinctive contribution of the Hebrew prophets to proclaim that the two cannot be rent apart; that men ought to treat each other as created in the image of God who challenges them" to do His will in the social order. He rejected alike "a secularism which bids religion mind its business, of which responsibility for the social order is to be no part, and an other-worldly religion which, accepting this advice, disclaims all responsibility for the social order." He noted that "secularist social morality has often put to shame a social morality supposedly religiously inspired," but "questioned whether secularist morality can, for long, treat men as created in the image of God in Whom it does not believe"—a question to which we must return. The Rabbi found difficulties for religion in seeking to discharge its responsibility in society. One of them concerns power. Refusing its use tended toward anarchy or "an amoral order based on naked power." But the use of power almost inevitably involves compromise, especially when one professes to wield power in the name of God. Hence Rabbi Fackenheim held that religion is confined to "indirect methods of pressure-by-exhortation. Here lies perhaps the deepest justification for the separation of church and state." He had observed earlier that separation of church and state is not at all the same thing as the divorce between the religious and social realms. For the believing attitude must "stubbornly insist on the will of God, not in general, or for some other place or time, but here and now. . . . The will of God is to be done in the social world of man; we are responsible for our share in it." Here again we find great emphasis on the responsibility of the laity.

Addressing a group of Protestant clergy and laymen in Portland, Maine, in October 1964, Dr. Robert S. Cohen, Chairman of the Physics Department of Boston University, suggested that the church stop speaking out on the nature and function of man "on which it has no right or ability to speak, comment in such fields being entirely the province of hard-headed science." One wonders whether Dr. Cohen would include Shakespeare, Dante as well as biblical writers in the category of those who are completely ignorant of the nature of man because they are not hard-headedly scientific. Dr. Cohen conceded that the church "does have a message for modern man . . . it is the message of the brotherhood of men—and that is enough." Dr. Cohen went on to criticize Christianity, Judaism and Islam as being unfit to lead modern man, charging that their beliefs are analogous to magic and that their doctrines have dealt with sin in terms of idolatry. Religion did not set out to be scientific, and is rather a-scientific than unscientific. Furthermore, if its transcendental premises are valid, sin *is* idolatry.

Dr. Cohen went on to indicate that one function of religion is to "stand as the critic of society." Here one of the grave difficulties in helping society to overcome its idolatries is that religion has burdened itself very generally through the centuries by harboring its own idolatries, such as literalism, clericalism, institutionalism and nativism. These beams in its own eyes must be removed if religion is to give valid aid to society in overcoming the idolatries which society caresses. This task also requires great perceptiveness. The virtue or the necessity of one age may become an antisocial anachronism in a later one. In an age of affluence, now at least visible on the horizon, cooperation both in producing and in sharing would be more valuable socially than competition. The spiritual perception of this possibility may prove to be just as necessary to its realization as the recognition which is reached through science and statistics.

It was also in October 1964 that Dr. Irvine H. Page, Director of Research at Cleveland Clinic, stated in an interview that science has been so successful in recent decades that more and more people look to it for answers even to transcendental questions. "But we don't have all the answers. Science will do all the research possible in this area, but it will remain objective and follow the rules of the game . . . value judgments don't have anything to do with science." Wisdom, Dr. Page felt, includes "the belief in something greater than we are—a transcendental life. . . . I think it is the happy combination of belief in religion and belief in materialism that makes one able to live as part of nature."

One must not overlook the fact that whatever contribution religion has to make through the positive and aggressive expression of its faith by groups and individuals, it also has a most important critical role to play. In the first place, it must be self-critical, searching always to distinguish its service to society and to men's deepest needs from self-service of religious bodies and their officials. It also has a wider critical function, of which society stands in great need. The consensus of some two hundred fifty scholars, scientists and churchmen attending a special consultation of leaders of religion in New York recently was to the effect that there is a deep need for religion "to become a judging and redemptive force in the society" (*Religious News Service,* March 3, 1965). This consensus was voiced by a consultation cosponsored by the Center for the Study of Democratic Institutions and the Fellowship of Reconciliation.

Included in the necessary self-criticism of religious bodies as they seek to influence the social order are two questions which they must constantly address to themselves. Are we spending so much energy on minor issues that the attention of our members and of the public is dulled when we need to raise major and urgent issues? Do we exercise care not to offend our friends and allies by a go-it-alone policy? If there is agreement, united action is more important, and more likely to be effective, than any prestige that might (and might not) accrue from unilateral action. If there is not agreement, it should be sought, and any insoluble differences should be expressed in a way to which the differing groups can agree.

Catholics, Jews and Protestants are anxious as to the possibility of the survival of the ethical fruits of religion if the roots should be neglected. This is a natural and a reasonable anxiety. The question whether the ethical values of secular humanism would survive without the continued functioning of theistic faith is one which could not be settled pragmatically until some generations after the cessation of the theistic witness. The debate is never likely to be settled theoretically; it has been going on for centuries. But it is not necessary for our purposes, even though one shares in the anxiety, that it be settled or further discussed. The question is rather, What should be the attitude of religious bodies and individuals toward a society that is in the constant process of secularization? This society as such is not likely to be greatly impressed by anxieties of the sort mentioned. But its response, its reactions may be greatly influenced by the attitudes, the stance, the patterns of religious response to secularization. Two patterns are distinguished by the Reverend Dean H. Lewis of the United Presbyterian Board of Education in a paper prepared early in 1965 for a dialogue group in Philadelphia:

The defensive and imperialist response to secularization sees the abandonment and rejection of "religion" as a categorical and ultimate threat. It acts on the assumption that what is being rejected or abandoned is real and vitally necessary to "religion." If the language patterns, concepts, forms, feelings, and action norms that are being diluted by secularization in both society and man are permitted to disappear completely, then "religion" will have disappeared—or at any rate "true religion." Naturally enough then, the response to secularization is resistance—an attempt to turn back the tide, to defend and maintain religion and reassert its influence over society and man—that is, to preserve and enlarge adherence to the modes of thought and action defined as religious. . . .

The missionary and adaptive response sees secularization more as a particular and transitory problem than a categorical and ultimate threat. It assumes that what is being rejected or abandoned is artificial and not necessarily vital to religion. This approach assumes that religion is constantly required to find new language patterns, concepts, forms and action norms for expressing its truth among men. It assumes that "secularization" is only the abandonment of certain formal expressions of religion and not religion itself. In other words, the missionary and adaptive approach assumes that the power and purpose and presence of God's action among men has not changed.

Perhaps once more theologians and the clergy in general are assuming, when they accept the burden of this anxiety, more responsibility than belongs to them. This is not to say that it is enough to proclaim the truth, or at least witness to one's own convictions, and assume that proper results will follow. There have always been, it is true, those who made just that assumption. To proclaim the truth is, indeed, the primary obligation of the clergy. It does not exempt them from participating in the social struggle at the side of lay men and women as counselors and as fellow citizens. But we should not in our anxiety forget that God may speak to the laity without benefit of clergy, and to the secular humanist without any official or designated religious spokesman as the medium. These are not considerations for the discounting of the religious witness—which after all is under an inner compulsion if it is authentic—but for the reassurance of the unduly anxious. The author was impressed as a boy by a cartoon, in a volume called *Character Sketches,* of the tiny figure of a Christian minister thrusting sturdily and anxiously against the "Rock of Ages" in the pious belief that it was his strength that supported it.

The primary danger, one must insist, is not that the churches may overestimate their responsibility in society, but that they may neglect or mistake it. One must be devoutly thankful that the Second Vatican Council has practically reversed what Dean Lewis styled the "defensive and imperialist response to secularization" of a century ago in favor of a "missionary and adaptive response." Time will be required to make the reversal effective throughout the Church. Meanwhile, one may hope that certain narrowly evangelical Protestants may begin to exchange the defensiveness of Pius IX for the expansiveness of John XXIII.

RELIGION AND POLITICS

It is not difficult to find examples of the influence of religion in politics, or at least of the mixture of religion and politics. Frequently the mixture has been beneficial neither to politics, to religion, nor to the social order. Constantine's official adoption of the Christian religion was probably quite beneficial to the empire in the short run. Marcus Aurelius, a century or so earlier, had refused that solution. He too saw clearly enough that an empire which depended upon the practical deification of the emperor could be undermined by any considerable body of believers who obstinately and openly refused even the formal recognition of such a deity. He could not sincerely accept the new faith, nor could he readily find an adequate political substitute for emperor worship. The menace to the empire, it is true, had greatly increased from the time of that great emperor and philosopher to the time of Constantine.

Religion and politics were again, and even more confusingly, intermingled in tension between Rome and Constantinople which culminated in the Great Schism of the eleventh century. Following the Protestant Reformation, there was a long period of religio-political wars. We see the religious element again in the cruel war between Spain and Holland, and in the struggle between Spain and Great Britain leading up to the defeat of the Invincible Armada. It was tragically manifest in the struggle for Irish independence, paralleled by Ulster's struggle for separation from Ireland. The effects of all these continue in one way or another to plague the Western world: they do not disappear, and sometimes even increase, with the signing of a treaty of peace. Isolation, persecution and genocide in the case of the Jews, a religio-ethnic phenomenon, frequently intermixed with an economic motive, sometimes involves also a political motivation and is inevitably attended with political consequences. Perhaps the proportions are reversed in the current strife between Cairo and Jerusalem, but all the elements seem to be present.

In our own country the religious factor in nineteenth century nativism and in the Ku Klux Klan of the past one hundred years must be acknowledged. Both have played more on religious and pseudo-religious emotions than on truly religious convictions. The sentiment enlisted in favor of laws prohibiting the production and sale of intoxicating drinks was based partly on genuine moral and religious conviction, partly on a kind of overweening self-righteousness, and partly on antagonism to newer elements in the national population for whom abstinence was not a necessary virtue: there were present thus both a positive and a negative religious factor. Both this prohibition sentiment and the anti-Catholicism so often included in nativism were factors in the defeat of Alfred E. Smith in the presidential campaign of 1928.

It is still difficult to say how large a part religion played, eight elections later, in electing President Kennedy. But without the efforts of Protestants, Catholics and Jews to distinguish religious motives from political preferences, anti-Catholicism might well have swung the close decision the other way. The damage that would have been done to politics and to society in that case is not to be sought in the continuation of one party or the other in power for a quadrennium: the issue with which we are here concerned would have been the same if it had been the Republican party that nominated a Catholic for President, and in fact there were men of both parties who strove to eliminate the anti-Catholic propaganda.

In spite of some horrible examples cited in preceding paragraphs, we still have to ask whether religion *should* influence politics, i.e., whether a beneficent influence upon politics can and should be exerted by religion, and if so, how. We do not at this point enter upon a discussion of the relations between church and state; for the moment, we simply assume the relationship, by no means static, to which we are accustomed in the United States.

In the United States the assumption seems to be general that religious divisions should not be emphasized and deepened by the organization of sectarian political parties. The situation is somewhat different in Europe. One may well imagine a situation where the political pressure of Communism within a country was so strong that all Catholics or all Christians or all theists—and many atheists—might feel it necessary to unite their votes in spite of their differences. This would be easier in Europe, where there is a certain heritage of parties supported, or even sponsored, by churches. On the whole, however, this tradition seems to be diminishing. The actions of the Vatican Council are not such as are likely to contribute to the revival of religious political parties. A device which may have helped to prevent the formation of such parties in this country is that of the balanced ticket. But the device itself is increasingly considered to be a nuisance if not a menace.

There is also encouraging evidence that in the United States a majority of all concerned—Protestants, Catholics, Jews and unaffiliated—are unwilling to undertake the imposition of their religio-moral convictions upon others through legislation or court action. Still less, of course, are they willing to have the convictions of others forced upon themselves by governmental action. We are still, however, involved in the experimental and, one hopes, learning process. In spite of the lesson of the failure of the Prohibition Amendment to the Constitution of the United States, we have not yet achieved the adjustments which are necessary and probably inevitable in the long run in a pluralist society, in such matters as Sunday closing laws, planned parenthood, censorship, betting parlors, divorce, adoption and the like, to some of which we shall return in a later chapter. The very process of adjustment can be a very wholesome one both for politics and for religion.

The prevailing opinion in the United States seems now to be that it is right and proper for those who have moral convictions to speak out and exert their influence in ways consistent with democratic procedures wherever and whenever a political issue involves a moral one. Some would say with Mr. Emerson Hynes, legislative assistant to Senator Eugene J. McCarthy, that there is not only a place but a need for skilled religious "petitioners" (the agreeable and constitutional term which he prefers to "lobbyists"). He observed at the Washington Institute:

> The history of all of Western civilization, our own culture included, speaks to us of the profound influence of religion on political structures and objectives. Judeo-Christian ideals —such as the nature and dignity of man, the rights of conscience, of individual and group responsibilities, the equality of all men before law—these are woven through Western culture. Continued effort is required to renew and advance these concepts.

Mr. Hynes felt at that time that while our religious groups have a splendid tradition for their moral witness, they too often leave their testimony to the broad principles of faith and give little help to the legislator who is struggling with a specific problem.

Part of the vagueness and timidity of our preachers may be laid to the belief that religion as such must not become involved in political controversy, or take on a partisan identity. However, it sometimes happens that there is really only one morally supportable side in a political controversy. Even when there is genuinely a moral question involved, the churches and synagogues in their pronouncements and their preachers in their sermons have an opportunity and a duty to weigh the respective considerations and help the "people of God" to act and to vote with well-instructed moral discrimination. Once more, while much of the burden rests upon the clergy and upon the community of faith as a whole, it is to laymen that we must look for specific and decisive political action.

While Jesus on some occasions avoided traps that had been cleverly contrived for him, both he and the Old Testament prophets spoke vigorously on matters that were primarily or secondarily political. Some of the prophets had to hide from the kings, or did not succeed in doing so. Some interpreters think that a plausible case can be made for the assertion that Jesus was executed for meddling in politics; an effort was made to convince Pilate of Jesus' political menace.

Because of our general respect for the pulpit, recalcitrant forces are constantly trying either to discredit its voice or to suborn it. The Klan has been known to exercise its influence by entering the sanctuary during a religious service, robed and hooded, and presenting a sizeable contribution for the religious ministry of the congregation. But this sort of negative influence is usually exercised in more subtle fashion.

When religious bodies conclude that pronouncements are necessary—which must not occur so often that they are accepted as routine and promptly forgotten—they must be careful to address their religious message to their own members, and their social and political challenge to the general body of citizens, with certain safeguards. One of these is not to claim a greater body of support for their message than can be substantiated. Another safeguard is to voice their moral convictions with no real or apparent assumption of moral superiority. Nor as a rule should the pronouncement opt for a particular legislative solution; it should aim simply to clarify the moral issues. A pronouncement may also help to avoid the choice of means which could only defeat the desired end. Care should be taken to assure full and open discussion.

Some state councils of churches exercise an educational function both for legislators and their constitutents. The Reverend Theodore L. Conklin has described the educational function of the New York State Council of Churches in this fashion:

> . . . We prepare and distribute each year to our legislature and people in our churches and our constituency, and others who are interested, a statement of legislative principles. It is a small thing but it represents, year after year, careful study by hundreds of church leaders who through it express their considered opinion on certain social and moral issues before our State legislature.
>
> Our church leaders and subscribers are then urged to communicate to their own legislators on their opinion, both as to the legislation and as to the Commission's position. . . . Legislators are advised to ask Protestants in their districts as to their opinion and are frequently told these people are their electors. . . . Frequently, legislators are reminded that we never speak for a total constituency, that there are always a number of our constituents who will disagree with us, but we believe them to be a minority, varying in number and in make-up with the particular issue. . . . We think, over a period of a decade or more now, this has been effective without exercising pressure or attempting to throw around a weight that we do not have.

RELIGION AND ECONOMICS

Speakers who were quoted earlier in this chapter as to the responsibility of religion in the social order all agreed that the churches' responsibility extends to the economic sphere. Rabbi Fackenheim said, "I cannot imagine an Amos alive today who would not involve himself in economic questions"—and most concretely, on the basis of the divine imperative. Amos, he said, would "talk to anybody in the pub and in the market place," religious or secularist.

In the nineteenth century there was wide agreement, with philosophical backing, that neither trade nor politics was within the same sphere as religion. It is highly probable that much of the support in the United States for the doctrine of church-state separation comes from those who assume that religion must be separate from both politics and economics. But there has been a steady stream of reaction, both Protestant and Catholic, against such circumscription of religion's relevance and obligation. It was not Karl Marx, but a Protestant clergyman and author, Charles Kingsley, who first pointed out the narcotizing effect of much of religion, making it opium rather than the dynamite that it might be, or the social leaven that it must be. In the United States Walter Rauschenbusch, Washington Gladden and a host of their followers began early in the present century to proclaim in pulpit and press the social implications of the Christian Gospel. Some denominations and the Federal Council of Churches formulated and proclaimed social creeds of the churches. Meanwhile kindred ideas were being proclaimed and propagated in three epoch-making papal encyclicals: Leo XIII's *Rerum Novarum* (1891), Pius XI's *Quadragesimo Anno* (1931) and John XXIII's *Mater et Magistra* (1962). Both Protestant and Catholic statements helped to support and guide the trade-union movement. Under the leadership of Methodist Bishop Francis J. McConnell and the Federal Council of Churches' report on the great steel strike of 1920, the inhumanity of the twelve-hour, six-day week became generally recognized; that and other abuses in industry began to be corrected. One might believe that the day for such reforms had arrived, and that they needed little help from the churches. This view is to a considerable extent belied by the criticism, ridicule and name-calling addressed to the churches and churchmen who called for and supported such reforms. One recalls also the markedly evangelical conviction and fervor of a number of the most conspicuous and effective labor leaders in Great Britain in the first half of the century. It is probably true that the churches cannot bring about a reform until circumstances facilitate it, but they can help to prepare the ground. Also, unfortunately, they can miss the day of their opportunity, as they too often have done.

The task of religion in economics is still an uphill one. There are still many who say, "Let the churches stick to religion," or when they fear that the churches and synagogues threaten to become really effective, cry, "Communism." A banker was quoted in the Washington Institute as having said that economically-illiterate clergy and churchly-illiterate politicians together could lead us straight down the road to Communism. Often such cries come from those who see their own interests threatened by the proclamations and activities of religious forces.

At the time of the textile strike during the '30's,—attended by widespread violence and a few fatalities, so that troops were called out in Georgia and both the Carolinas—a Fellowship of Reconciliation pamphlet, "Can Guns Settle Strikes?", was labeled "Communist" by the *Southern Textile Bulletin,* although the pamphlet was based on careful research and was sponsored by a group of the foremost educational and religious leaders of the South.

Rabbi Aaron Decter, in a paper prepared for a local discussion group in March 1965, finds that "the dividing line between the spheres of religion and secular business is shifting. . . . It is increasingly evident that ethical idealism and economic interests, or moral integrity and political interests, are no longer safely locked up in separate compartments." This is partly due to the fact that we seem to be on the threshold of the affluent society. This may help society to realize that certain forms of competition are no longer necessary, and indeed have been largely antisocial both in their spirit and in their result.

Secular forces may be relied upon in the comparatively short run to increase production to the level of a decent life, with two provisos: that the increase is not cancelled out by the increase in population, and that the products are used fairly for the benefit of all. Religious forces can aid by finding and promoting moral methods of family planning and by working constantly for fair wages, job training and international economic cooperation.

Religion's task in the economic field meets the inherent difficulty of adapting its own message and social habits in general to changing conditions; it also meets the inertia and resistance of many of its adherents, who first cannot be convinced, and then are reluctant or unwilling to act. Their reluctance is in part human resistance to the change of old habits, and in part unwillingness to sacrifice what seem to be one's personal interests to what is only dimly seen as the general good. An excellent illustration is found in the current campaigns on the part of churches and synagogues and their individual leaders for open occupancy in housing. Sermons and resolutions boldly, forcefully and intelligently conceived and delivered have by no means achieved the results intended and hoped for. They seem to have been more successful in producing legislative enactments, where one deals with a few individuals, than in producing majorities in a referendum, where one votes anonymously and as part of a mass.

The involvement of Western religious leaders and their followers in an unremitting campaign against Communism is attended by two dangers. Dr. Alan Walker, noted Australian Methodist, said recently that "Christianity has failed to distinguish between the evil about Communism and the good for which it strives. . . . The Christian Church in the main has maneuvered into the position where it denies the hope of millions for greater economic justice, and into the position where it appears to endorse and entrench the injustice of capitalism." It would indeed be unfortunate if Western religion relinquished the criticism of capitalism, necessary to its constant readjustment and refinement, to Communist critics, as ready to throw out the good in capitalism as we often seem ready to throw out the good along with the bad in Communism. Unqualified defense of capitalism and denunciation of Communism also obstruct the dialogue which has begun and is increasing, at least informally and unofficially, in many places between Christians and Communists. The National Council of Churches and the World Council of Churches have promoted exchanges of church delegations between capitalist and Communist countries. This exchange helps toward the understanding that Christians have a function to perform when they are citizens in a Communist society, plus the recognition of the simple fact that there are Christians in such societies. Less official discussions, particularly concerning international questions, are increasing in frequency and in importance. Even so, it may well be that scientists and business men are progressing faster in bringing about a tolerable coexistence between Russia and the United States than are the religious leaders. The Vatican has made some interesting moves in acknowledging the need and the possibility of dialogue between Christians and Communists. The Vatican Council made it plain in various documents that atheist, materialist, totalitarian concepts and institutions are incompatible with Christianity. It could therefore refuse the plea of nearly three hundred bishops—about fifteen of them from the United States—that an explicit condemnation of Communism should be adopted.

One sees occasionally, on the part of Communists and in Communist publications, appeals to recognize the good or at least the goodness in Christianity and to lower the barriers between the two cultures and the two societies. Such portents are still infrequent and far from massive in their impact, but may well prove to be, from the two sides, a most important element in bringing a stable coexistence to the Western world—which in turn could not fail to have some influence in the Asiatic world.

Both Christians and Jews maintain relations and exchange visits with their co-religionists behind the Iron Curtain; even these actions are fiercely criticized as at least "softness" on Communism. But these contacts could be widened as to numbers involved, and broadened as to scope, to the great reinforcement of peaceful coexistence, and with important, perhaps determinative, influence on cooperation in the elimination of poverty and war.

3

RELIGIOUS LIBERTY

The development of the doctrine of religious liberty and its increasing acceptance and application is a gift to society of fundamental importance: it is due in no small measure to religious forces. And religious liberty is an indispensable condition for religion's maximum contribution to society.

What is religious liberty? How important is it? A chapter will not answer those questions, but it may serve as a guide, an introduction. At the outset we note Walter Lippman's assertion of some years ago that the final resistance to tyranny in all the totalitarian regimes has been made by devoutly religious churchmen. We note also Cardinal Koenig's statement as member of a panel in Rome, in December 1965, that religion has a certain function as society's critical conscience. Woe to society if it stifles its conscience!

It was not surprising that many thoughtful churchmen, of all three major Christian confessions, named the Vatican Council's statement on religious liberty as its outstanding action or as its key contribution to aggiornamento, a sine qua non of further ecumenical development. Keeping in mind the general significance of freedom of conscience, we turn to its role in our own history.

Relationships developed in the United States constitutionally, between church and state, and pragmatically, between religious bodies and government, constitute probably the most conspicuous American contribution to political jurisprudence, and the surest foundation for freedom of conscience and of worship in a pluralist society.

43

The Federal Council of Churches (Protestant) in 1944 issued this statement:

> The separation of church and state has been our great bulwark of religious freedom in America. It has insured a policy of equal treatment of all religious bodies by the national government. It has afforded to every church an equal opportunity to develop its inherent possibilities. It has thereby provided a spiritual climate favorable to goodwill and co-operation among Protestants, Roman Catholics and Jews.

Just what separation is and implies we shall see as we go along; we note here that it is generally agreed that we do not have an absolute separation, and that it is indeed for both theoretical and practical considerations not to be contemplated. Furthermore, the separation of church and state is only a favoring condition of religious liberty, not a guarantee. As we have seen, in Tsarist Russia church and state were very closely tied together. The Eastern Orthodox Church enjoyed probably as much freedom as it desired, given the fact that its chief concerns were for worship and other matters that might be called internal. But neither it nor the state granted very much liberty to other religious bodies. The Y.M.C.A., for example, which the author frequented in 1916-17 in Petrograd (now Leningrad) had to be called The Lighthouse (Mayak). The U.S.S.R. today professes constitutionally church-state separation and religious liberty, but there are continuing and disturbing evidences of discrimination against both Jews and Christians.

In both eastern European and Moslem countries there is traditionally so close an identification of state, people and religion that the question of separation of church and state scarcely arose until quite recently, partly under the general and worldwide impact of pluralism, and partly because of the ideological rejection of religion under Communist regimes. This tradition of identity helps to account for a resistance on the part of the Orthodox Church in Greece both to evangelizing agencies of other Christian bodies and to the ecumenical feelers put out by the Vatican. After World War II the author was entrusted with small relief funds for Christian students in Italy who were refugees or prisoners of war: a Yugoslav Moslem pleaded that he should not be excluded simply because he happened to have been born in a Moslem area of his country: born in a Christian province, he would have been a Christian!

The same kind of identification was prevalent in western Europe until the Reformation, and survived for a time in the maxim and the practice that the religion of the king would determine the religion of the people. The notion survives to a greater or lesser degree wherever there is an established church; rather more, for example, in Spain and in Sweden, rather less in England.

In England, in fact, establishment is consistent with a large degree of religious liberty. It is the Church of England itself that suffers from restrictions of its own liberties because of establishment; there are very few restrictions on other religious bodies, though their bishops, if they have them, are not automatically members of the House of Lords, and they do not receive automatically the same sort of financial support as does the established church. In the revision of the proposed Vatican Council declaration on religious liberty there was inserted, after the 1963 session, a brief paragraph to the effect that establishment is not necessarily a limitation of religious liberty. The paragraph was retained in the final version adopted in 1965.

As a part of our search for those relations between church and state which are consistent with religious liberty, we need to inquire what religious liberty is and how it is related to religious freedom and distinguished from it. The theist, believing that God created man in His own image and continues to be concerned with him, affirms that freedom is a God-given right, an essential attribute of man, an inherent right of the human being as such; and the theist goes on to say that religious freedom is the most intimate and the

most essential of all freedoms, basic in fact. The nonreligious humanist would probably agree that where there is no religious freedom, other freedoms are likely to be incomplete, if not as a consequence, at least as an accompaniment of the absence of religious
freedom.

Freedom, as an inherent God-given attribute of human beings,
since it is subjective and interior, is indestructible, capable of
maintaining itself against all tyrants. Thousands, perhaps millions,
of martyrs to their faith are unimpeachable witnesses to this invincibility ("martyr" signifies witness); not all of them are in the
Judeo-Christian tradition. This inherent interior freedom is not
bestowed by the state; governments cannot take it away. When
governments attempt to do so, it is tyranny. When, on the other
hand, the state constitutionally and the government operationally
recognize, respect, guarantee and protect the outward manifesta-
tion of religion, we have religious liberty, a juridical phenomenon.
(There are other approaches to religious liberty, to which some
reference will be made; this one seems to prevail increasingly.)

The definition and justification of religious liberty by religious
bodies in terms that will satisfy their theologians, and give the
secular state a rational basis for maintaining it, is not a task for the
novice. The then newly consolidated National Council of the
Churches of Christ in the U.S.A., feeling the necessity of a statement, in 1954 adopted the following, somewhat pragmatic one,
submitted to its General Board by the Department of Religious
Liberty (the author was at that time the Department's Executive
Director):

> Religious liberty and indeed religious faith are basic both
> historically and philosophically to all our liberties.

> The National Council of Churches holds the first clause of
> the First Amendment to the Constitution of the United States
> to mean that church and state shall be separate and inde-
> pendent as institutions, but to imply neither that the state is

indifferent to religious interests nor that the church is indifferent to civic and political issues.

The National Council of Churches defends the rights and liberties of cultural, racial and religious minorities. The insecurity of one menaces the security of all. Christians must be especially sensitive to the oppression of minorities.

The exercise of both rights and liberties is subject to considerations of morality and to the maintenance of public order and of individual and collective security.

Religious and civil liberties are interdependent and therefore indivisible.

The National Council of Churches urges the churches, because of their concern for all human welfare, to resist every threat to freedom.

The Congregational Christian Churches (now a part of the United Church of Christ) said in 1948 that the principle of separation was not intended to silence the church on public questions, or to relieve the state of moral responsibility. Both church and state, they said, are subject to God's laws, and each must cooperate with the other in discerning and obeying these laws in human community.

We quote from a Lutheran statement made in Alexandria, Virginia, in 1953:

As Luther interpreted the Scriptures, there are two divine kingdoms . . . a spiritual and a secular . . . God rules in both kingdoms . . . on the right . . . his Church by the Gospel . . . on the left . . . by the Law. . . . Separation of church and state in America does not have the "absolute" connotation . . . [which] denies the function of the Christian community to be the salt of the earth and the light shining in darkness.

Roman Catholics have frequently referred to the two swords, one wielded by the temporal power, the other by the spiritual power. In the 1950's an internationally known Catholic was a candidate in southern Germany for the West German Parliament, and not on the ticket favored by his church. His archbishop remonstrated with him, but he appealed to the doctrine of the two swords, continued his candidacy, and was elected.

The Lutheran and Catholic approaches are similar in purport to the parable of the two olive trees in the vision in the fourth chapter of Zechariah, cited and interpreted by Rabbi Arthur Gilbert in an address, in May 1965, before the World Congress of the Catholic Press. The prophet sees a seven-branched golden candlestick, the Menorah, which has an unfailing supply of oil, supplied by two olive trees representing prince and priest, the civic and religious leaders of the community. Thus, said Rabbi Gilbert, "It is made clear that God acts upon His people with munificent love, through both political and religious instrumentalities. Both are vessels of His will and come under His judgment." Thus State and Religion are not to be arbitrarily separated from each other.

In the words of Lord Acton, quoted in *The Commonweal,* May 1, 1953: "In politics as in science the Church need not seek her own ends. She will obtain them if she encourages the pursuit of the ends of science, which are truth, and of the State, which are liberty."

Luigi Luzzatti, an Italian Jewish philosopher, held that the coordination of ends of faith and science could be effected only by liberty, as they now diverge, now meet, and now contradict each other. "History," he said, "has already judged with infallible answers, and it has condemned those who lay their hands upon science in the name of God, or upon God in the name of science; and the doctrine of organic and constitutional liberty does not draw its reason only from the innermost recesses of conscience, but finds in history its most effectual sanctions and most evident consecration." We shall return to the historical sources of religious liberty later in this chapter. As to conscience, church statements tend to take it for granted: its nature and authority merit further study.

It would seem to be clear from the foregoing that there is and can be no absolute separation between church and state, still less between religion and government. But there should be no inter-meshing of gears between the institutions of government and those of religion. To avoid intermeshing, there must be, of course, no domination of the church by the state, nor of the state by the church. The necessary separation, which is embodied in the Con-stitution and interpreted in countless judicial decisions, involves constant and vigilant distinguishing between the powers and the instruments of the sacred authorities and those of the secular au-thorities.

Our whole experience goes to teach us that there must be coop-eration of some kind, but in limited degree, between governmental and religious forces if we are to make life tolerable for citizens who are also members of churches or synagogues, and if we are to avoid two rather contrary dangers to religion (if religion serves society usefully, a danger to religion is also a danger to society). One danger is that the doctrine of separation may be pushed to a point where we have not so much freedom for religion as freedom from religion. A great many persons felt that the Supreme Court was approaching this danger in a series of decisions extending from the McCollum Case, Champaign, Illinois, 1948, to the 1962 and 1963 decisions barring prayer and devotional Bible reading from the official activities of public schools. (See further Chapter 4.) Many, especially among Protestants, are greatly concerned, on the other hand, lest governmental support, moral and financial, be accepted by religious bodies and institutions to the point where their independence is seriously jeopardized.

SOURCES AND SUPPORT OF RELIGIOUS LIBERTY

There are those who seek no sources for religious liberty outside of religion itself, and others who give an overwhelming preponderance of credit to contributions from secular forces. We quote some evidence of both sorts, but not with any expectation that we can or should arrive at a verdict in the controversy. It is important to give credit where credit is due. If we are to preserve, extend and refine religious liberty, we need to know and to understand all that we can of its origins, and consequently, one may hope, what forces can be relied upon in the continuing struggle. Much of the testimony in favor of a secular origin is from Jews and nonreligious humanists—who, however, in each case that we shall cite, are identified as foremost friends and supporters of religious liberty. Rabbi Bertram Korn found that the legal status of Judaism, the only non-Christian faith which is well rooted in American society, is probably a more accurate index of religious freedom than any other: "from the perspective of history, it is an intellectual and spiritual achievement of no little significance for Christians to regard dissenting co-religionists as brother Christians of erring or differing views, rather than as enemies. But for Christians to be lovingly responsive to the appeal of Jews—descendants of those who rejected the Christian Saviour—that they are also brothers, is a far more difficult challenge." He held that Jews and Judaism enjoy a closer approximation of religious freedom and equality in the United Sates than in any other country of the Western world at any time in history. The rabbi found that the juridical achievement of religious liberty is more to the credit of secularists than of religious bodies or their spokesmen, who sometimes stood against equal recognition of the Jewish religion in civic matters, such as chaplaincy for legislatures and the armed forces. President Lincoln, in fact, had to intervene in order to amend the Act of Congress in 1861 which approved as chaplains for the army "regularly ordained ministers of some Christian denomination." The Jewish chaplain commissioned under the Amended Act, September 1862, was the first to be so commissioned anywhere in the world. While many Christians joined with Jews in the campaign for amendment, the only official Christian voices were negative. Jews, Rabbi Korn reported, were more daring and more active in seeking to bring about religious equality before the law than they had been in other countries because of their faith in America as representing a new start in the life of the world. Was their faith in America, however, not due in large part to the work of religionists like Roger Williams, William Penn and Lord Baltimore?

In a Jewish-Catholic Institute of NCCJ's Project on "Religious Freedom and Public Affairs" at Latrobe, Pennsylvania, January 1965, Rabbi Robert Gordis also voiced the opinion that the "ideal of religious liberty is essentially a gift we owe to the secularists. . . . By and large, the principle of freedom of conscience became widely held and increasingly operative only with the age of reason." But Rabbi Gordis discounts such support for religious liberty as inadequate, tending toward the opinion that one religion is as good—or as bad—as another, raising the question by implication whether the toleration of something that doesn't really matter is to be equated with liberty for something that matters supremely. Mere toleration, indeed, is not to be equated with a genuine affirmation of religious liberty; this accounts in large part for the struggle that went on within the Roman Catholic Church over the declaration on religious liberty in the Second Vatican Council.

Rabbi Gordis notes three aspects or stages in the evolution of a doctrine and practice of religious freedom within a religion, and holds that the Jewish religion has made conspicuous contributions to each: the claim to freedom for oneself; the extension of freedom of conscience to religious bodies that differ in belief and practice; and the grant of freedom of thought and action to dissidents within its own ranks.

Prof. Sidney Hook, a secular humanist, upholds religious liberty from the viewpoint of the open society. But, he said, an open democratic society "does not rest on any religious or metaphysical presuppositions." He denied that "moral values are logically dependent upon transcendent religious beliefs" unless "moral predicates have been surreptitiously introduced" into the existential predicates. Belief in the brotherhood of man under the fatherhood of God, he held, is not a *sufficient* condition of democracy.

Referring to Mr. Justice Douglas' dictum in *Zorach vs. Clauson* (1952), "We are a religious people whose institutions presuppose a Supreme Being," Prof. Hook accepts as a historic fact that we are a religious people, but can draw no Constitutional consequences from it. "The statement that our institutions presuppose the existence of a Supreme Being is a much more momentous assertion . . . it asserts that the validity of the institutions which constitute the American way of life depends upon the existence of a Supreme Being as a necessary condition." If that could be established, Professor Hook thinks, then believers in the democratic state should publicly encourage and support religious belief and practice, and those critical of the belief would be trying to undermine democracy. "Religious tolerance has developed more," says Professor Hook, "as a consequence of the impotence of religions to impose their dogmas on each other, than as a consequence of spiritual humility in the quest for understanding first and last things."

We wonder whether, and how far, Prof. Hook would discount the spiritual humility of William Penn, who in the seventeenth century brought religious liberty to Pennsylvania. Roger Williams may have been more obstinate than humble, but he went a long way into Rabbi Gordis' second category of seeking liberty for others, and of resisting the Massachusetts authorities who would not permit dissidents in their own ranks. It is true that many of the pre-Reformation and Reformation witnesses and martyrs for religious liberty belonged in the rabbi's first category, but their contribution to the development of *religious* liberty is surely more important than that of those secularists who were interested only in liberty and regarded religion as at best a nuisance in society, and at worst a danger. But again we must remember, as Prof. Hook also remarked, that friends of freedom do not have to agree in their explanations and motivations in order to join in maintaining it.

Religious pluralism and religious liberty developed together in the colonial and early federal eras in the United States. When the time came to write a Federal Constitution, it was obvious that there could be no single established church for the nation; no one entertained the absurd idea of a multiple establishment nationally; hence our First Amendment prohibited, on the one hand, legislation tending toward an establishment of religion and, on the other, legislation interfering with the free exercise of religion. It seems undeniable that many of the statesmen who supported religious liberty at that time did so on the ground that religion is a private matter. In one sense, of course, this is true; that is, a person's religious beliefs and attitudes, including his belief in a Supreme Being, are not subject to the full knowledge and understanding of any other person or persons, and are still less subject to outside interference. The whole tenor of this book, however, and continuing and increasing evidences from our own and world history, accord with the view that while a person's religion is essentially private, it exerts an influence on society, particularly when multitudes of persons act together to bring their beliefs to bear upon social institutions and behavior.

Msgr. John Tracy Ellis, in the Washington Institute, observed that "the ideas that shaped the future development of American religious life and practice did not originate in Santa Fe or Monterey, or New Orleans or Detroit, but rather in Williamsburg, Boston and Philadelphia . . . from the English and their descendants," but he recorded various and important Catholic contributions to the development of religious liberty in the United States. The first American archbishop, John Carroll of Baltimore, foresaw that America might "come to exhibiting proof to the world that general and equal toleration, by giving a free circulation to free argument, is the most effectual method to bring all denominations of Christians to a unity of faith." Here we see the beginning in Carroll's ideas of liberty, dialogue, and ecumenism.

Even in Ireland, Bishop Edward Nolan of Kildare in 1835, in a conversation with de Tocqueville, opposed any link between church and state, and particularly any financial dependence of the church on the government. It was his views, according to Msgr. Ellis, which prevailed among the Irish of the great exodus to America. American prelates quoted to the same intent by Msgr. Ellis include the first bishop of Charleston, John England, and John Hughes, the first archbishop of New York.

Archbishop John Purcell of Cincinnati left the First Vatican Council before the vote on infallibility, but he uttered after his return what he had intended to say in the Council, a strong testimony to the "perfect liberty to every denomination of Christians" granted by the Constitution of the United States. In general, according to Msgr. Ellis, the Catholic ideology in the United States reflects the "American milieu." He quotes an American archbishop as having said in 1962 that if the Second Vatican Council did nothing else than to declare in favor of universal religious freedom, it would fully justify itself. The American bishops testified just prior to the Second Vatican Council to "the advantages which have come to the church from living and growing in an atmosphere of religious and political freedom. The very struggle which the church here has had to face has been responsible in large measure for the vitality which it has developed as it grew to maturity, unaided by political preference but unimpeded by political ties."

The Council's "Declaration on Religious Freedom" begins with "the dignity of the human person," and the increasing demand by contemporary men that coercion give way to "responsible freedom." The Church finds this demand to be in harmony with its own tradition and doctrine, which it holds to be derived from God Himself. "We believe that this one true religion subsists in the catholic and apostolic Church . . . all men are bound to seek the truth, especially in what concerns God and His Church, and to embrace the truth they come to know, and to hold fast to it." Christians who regularly recite their belief in the "catholic" Church may readily accept the first part of this quotation, where catholic is written with a small "c." Most Protestants, however, and many Catholics, regard the paragraph as a whole as an inef-

fectual attempt to win over conservative bishops, and agree that
the implication of Rome's exclusive possession of the truth is, as
Father Tavard of Pittsburgh, a member of the bishops' press panel,
said to American newsmen, out of place in this Declaration. This
only dims, it does not quench, the light and hope of the Declaration, from which we cite other excerpts:

> This Vatican Council likewise professes its belief that it is
> upon the human conscience that these obligations fall and
> exert their binding force. The truth cannot impose itself ex-
> cept by virtue of its own truth. . . . Religious freedom . . . has
> to do with immunity from coercion in civil society. . . .

> The right to religious freedom has its foundation, not in the
> subjective disposition of the person, but in his very nature.
> In consequence, the right to this immunity continues to exist
> even in those who do not live up to their obligation of seeking
> the truth and adhering to it and the exercise of this right
> is not to be impeded, provided that just public order be ob-
> served.

> On his part, man perceives and acknowledges the imperatives
> of the divine law through the mediation of conscience. In all
> his activity a man is bound to follow his conscience, in order
> that he may come to God, the end and purpose of life. It
> follows that he is not to be forced to act in a manner contrary
> to his conscience. Nor, on the other hand, is he to be re-
> strained from acting in accordance with his conscience, espe-
> cially in matters religious. The reason is that the exercise of
> religion, of its very nature, consists before all else in those
> internal, voluntary, and free acts whereby man sets the
> course of his life directly toward God. No merely human
> power can either command or prohibit acts of this kind. The
> social nature of man, however, itself requires that he should
> give external expression to his internal acts of religion: that

he should share with others in matters religious: that he should profess his religion in community. Injury therefore is done to the human person and to the very order established by God for human life, if the free exercise of religion is denied in society, provided just public order is observed.

The freedom or immunity from coercion in matters religious which is the endowment of persons as individuals is also to be recognized as their right when they act in community. . . .

The family, since it is a society in its own original right, has the right freely to live its own domestic religious life under the guidance of parents. Parents, moreover, have the right to determine, in accordance with their own religious beliefs, the kind of religious education that their children are to receive . . . the rights of parents are violated, if their children are forced to attend lessons or instruction which are not in agreement with their religious beliefs, or if a single system of education, from which all religious formation is excluded, is imposed upon all.

The care of the right to religious freedom devolves upon the whole citizenry, upon social groups, upon government, and upon the Church and other religious communities, in virtue of the duty of all toward the common welfare, and in the manner proper to each.

If, in view of peculiar circumstances obtaining among peoples, special civil recognition is given to one religious community in the constitutional order of society, it is at the same time imperative that the right of all citizens and religious communities to religious freedom should be recognized and made effective in practice.

Society has the right to defend itself against possible abuses committed on pretext of freedom of religion. It is the special duty of government to provide this protection. . . . Its action is to be controlled by juridical norms which are in conformity with the objective moral order.

The Declaration of this Vatican Council on the right of man to religious freedom has its foundation in the dignity of the person, whose exigencies have come to be more fully known to human reason through centuries of experience. What is more, this doctrine of freedom has roots in divine revelation, and for this reason Christians are bound to respect it all the more conscientiously.

It is one of the major tenets of Catholic doctrine that man's response to God in faith must be free: no one therefore is to be forced to embrace the Christian faith against his own will. This doctrine is contained in the word of God and it was constantly proclaimed by the Fathers of the Church. The act of faith is of its very nature a free act.

There follows, in the Declaration, support for religious freedom from the words and the deeds of Jesus and of the Apostles. There is also, along with the Church's record of faithfulness, a confession: "there has at times appeared a way of acting that was hardly in accord with the spirit of the Gospel, or even opposed to it. Nevertheless, the doctrine of the Church that no one is to be coerced into faith has always stood firm." And there is the declaration of the Church's need for freedom in order to carry on her mission of redemption.

Neither Protestants nor Catholics can contemplate with calm what would have been the effect in the United States of the Vatican Council's failure to promulgate a strong declaration in favor of religious liberty. In addition, such a failure would have been a reversal of the tendency embodied in the Council's most important actions in the first three sessions on the nature of the church, the liberalization of liturgical practices, and the decree on ecumenism:

religious liberty is an inescapable logical and historical corollary of the Council's actions.

Dr. W. A. Visser t'Hooft, General Secretary of the World Council of Churches, speaking in May 1965 before the General Board of the National Council of Churches, expressed his conviction that the chief import of the declaration would not be its probable effect on religious minorities around the world, but rather the fact that it would signalize and give evidence of the Roman Catholic return to the idea of the *corpus Christianum,* the Christian body.

In Protestant Europe both the Reformation and the reformers laid important foundations and made important contributions to religious liberty: Waldensians, Calvinists, Lutherans, Anabaptists, Socinians (Unitarians), Moravians, Mennonites, Huguenots, Baptists, Congregationalists, Quakers and Methodists.

In this country during the colonial period, among the most important forerunners of our present views and policies in religious liberty and separation of church and state were Roger Williams, William Penn and Lord Baltimore. Roger Williams denounced religious wars as contrary to Scripture and to the Prince of Peace; exposed the guilt in any persecution of conscience; held that the only sword justified in such a warfare is that of the spirit; urged civil statesmen to keep to civil matters; declared that God requires no government-imposed uniformity of belief, since the imposition denies both civil and Christian principle; demonstrated that toleration is necessary for peace, and is not inimical to civil and religious welfare. In the colony which he founded toleration was wide enough to include both Roman Catholics and Jews. For him religious liberty was not the gift of the state, but something retained by the people when they constituted the state. (Political disability for Roman Catholics was introduced in Rhode Island for a period following the English Acts of Toleration of 1689.)

The next most liberal of the colonies was William Penn's charter colony in Pennsylvania. By 1776 only one-fifth of the congregations were Quakers, i.e., members of Penn's faith. There were then ten different Protestant denominations and nine Catholic parishes.

Penn himself wrote often and consistently in behalf of separation of church and state, and respect for the individual conscience, which he held to be of the essence of the Christian message. He suffered much in England because of his heterodox views.

Catholic Cecil Calvert, Lord Baltimore, brought about Maryland's Act of Toleration for all Trinitarians in 1649, for "the peaceable government of the province . . . the better to preserve mutual love and amity among the inhabitants." Ratification by the colony's assembly of freemen, at least half of whom were Catholics, was required to make the Act effective.

But generally the free exercise of religion in the States began only at the time of the War of Independence. North Carolina and Georgia enacted disestablishing declarations in 1776 and '77, and the others soon followed, except Connecticut and Massachusetts; in the latter, disestablishment came only in 1833. However, the practice of toleration lagged well behind its proclamation, and so embodied various disabilities for Jews (even in Pennsylvania) and Catholics. In Virginia James Madison and George Mason were pressing for religious liberty as early as 1776; George Washington and Patrick Henry were among those who believed that an established church was a necessity for an orderly society. Madison, be it noted, was influenced by Witherspoon of Princeton, a religious leader. By 1786, with the additional help of Thomas Jefferson, the party of liberty was able to secure the adoption of the Great Bill for Religious Freedom:

> No man shall be compelled to frequent or support any religious worship, place, or ministry, whatsoever, nor shall suffer on account of his religious opinions or belief; opinions in matters of religion shall in no wise diminish, enlarge, or affect civic capacities. The rights hereby asserted are of the natural rights of mankind.

"This," says Professor Littell, "was the first time in history that a state which possessed the power and authority to establish and enforce religious orthodoxy, deliberately turned—not to toleration, which is prudent, but to liberty, which is noble. The Virginia experience had a shaping influence on the adoption of the First Amendment to the Federal Constitution. Here was more than the civic prudence of secularism, namely, the *theological* conviction of the inviolability of the human conscience. North Carolina and Rhode Island refused to join the Union without protection for civil and religious liberties. The Rhode Island resolution spoke of the 'natural, equal and unalienable right to the exercise of religion according to the dictates of conscience.' "

Early in this chapter a statement on religious liberty by the National Council of Churches was quoted. The World Council of Churches, with which are affiliated over two hundred Protestant and Orthodox bodies, has made various statements in support of religious liberty and is moving toward a more comprehensive one. In the excerpts from recent statements which we quote below, one will note many similarities with the Vatican Council statement. These excerpts are from statements by the World Council of Churches from 1948, when its constituting assembly met in Amsterdam, to its third full meeting at New Delhi in 1961:

The most fundamental freedom is religious freedom.

Every person has the right to determine his own faith and creed.

Religious liberty may be considered as a distinctive human right, which all men may exercise no matter what their faith.

Freedom to manifest one's religion or belief, in public or in private and alone or in community with others, is essential to the expression of inner freedom.

Every person has the right to express his religious beliefs in worship, teaching and practice, and to proclaim the implications of his beliefs for relationships in a social or political community.

It is presumptuous for the state to assume that it can grant or deny fundamental rights.

Only the recognition that man has ends and loyalties beyond the state will ensure true justice to the human person.

Human attempts by legal enactment or by pressure of social custom to coerce or to eliminate faith are violations of the fundamental ways of God with men.

The community has the right to require obedience to non-discriminatory laws passed in the interest of public order and well-being. In the exercise of its rights, a religious organization must respect the rights of other religious organizations and must safeguard the corporate and individual rights of the entire community.

It appears that the World Council statement now in process of development will also place great emphasis on religious liberty as something which the state owes, and guarantees to religion. The World Council will also probably continue to pay more attention to freedom of conscience within the church as an essential part of religious liberty than the Vatican Council has done in its Declaration. The National Council of Churches, in fact, treats the denial of freedom of conscience within a church as an infringement of religious liberty not essentially different from its infringement by the state. There are delicate questions here as to how far freedom of conscience is compatible with continuing membership in a church with which one disagrees at essential points: religious liberty could be consistent either with the member's voluntary withdrawal or his excommunication. The question of freedom within the church is probably more difficult for Roman Catholics than for Protestants. One heard that Roman Catholic misgivings on this point, even at a very high level, extended to the declaration itself, with the fear that any such declaration would encourage heterodoxy and lack of discipline. It is difficult to understand why an appeal to governments to respect the rights of conscience should encourage adherents of a faith to revolt against it. But any attempts to deal with intra-church freedom in the Council Declaration would almost certainly have raised enough ecclesiastical and theological questions to prevent a clear consensus for it. (Advances in intra-church freedom were made by other actions of the Vatican Council.)

A kindred misgiving regards the assumed or implied justification, by any affirmation of religious liberty, of the propagation of a false religion. But here again the objection seems fallacious if religious liberty is treated as something which the state is asked to recognize and protect, for the churches cannot afford to ask or permit governments to be the judges of what constitutes false religion—or even of what constitutes religion.

The invincibility of internal or subjective religious freedom is subject to two modifications, one historical and one modern. Probably those martyrs who resisted to the death were, in almost any period to be chosen, in the minority. Furthermore, it is possible to "martyrize," to exterminate believers to the point where no witnesses are left, as seems to have happened to Christians in one period of Japanese history, and to Protestants at another period in Spain. In modern times the possibility of "brainwashing" may prove to be a formidable limitation on resistance to tyranny on religious as well as on other grounds.

Comparison of the development of religious liberty among both Protestants and Catholics tends to confirm the thesis that in each case the first step was toleration, and only after successive steps was genuine religious liberty attained.

Dr. Carillo de Albornoz, religious liberty staff specialist for the

World Council of Churches, comments that while the whole world is verbally and theoretically committed to religious liberty, the practice varies widely with regard to its application and protection. This argues for him a difference of understanding of what religious liberty is, and this in turn is sometimes due to the vagueness of definition by statute or constitution. The variations in any case are such as to render it very important for theistic thinkers, and for the churches and synagogues, to arrive at substantial agreement as to the meaning of religious liberty.

Closely related to the need for agreement on the meaning of religious liberty is the need for a common understanding of what is meant by conscience. The National Council of Churches has seen this need, and is undertaking studies to meet it. The need has been recently illustrated by a decision of the Supreme Court of the United States with regard to the exemption of conscientious objectors from military service, or their assignment to alternate service to society. The Vatican Council rather took "conscience" for granted in its Declaration on Religious Liberty. In the *Constitution on the Church in the Modern World,* however, there is a paragraph on conscience, in the context of man's intellect, wisdom, and the aid of the Holy Spirit (division 16):

> In the depths of his conscience, man detects a law which he does not impose upon himself, but which holds him to obedience. Always summoning him to love good and avoid evil, the voice of conscience when necessary speaks to his heart: do this, shun that. For man has in his heart a law written by God; to obey it is the very dignity of man; according to it he will be judged. Conscience is the most secret core and sanctuary of a man. There he is alone with God, Whose voice echoes in his depths. In a wonderful manner conscience reveals that law which is fulfilled by love of God and neighbor. In fidelity to conscience, Christians are joined with the rest of men in the search for truth, and for the genuine solution to the numerous problems which arise in the life of individuals

and from social relationships. Hence the more right conscience holds sway, the more persons and groups turn aside from blind choice and strive to be guided by the objective norms of morality. Conscience frequently errs from invincible ignorance without losing its dignity. The same cannot be said for a man who cares but little for truth and goodness, or for a conscience which by degrees grows practically sightless as a result of habitual sin.

Paragraph 17 then begins, "Only in freedom can man direct himself towards goodness."

It should be noted that one difficulty faced by religious bodies in defining religious liberty is the matter of proselytism. It is difficult for those bodies themselves to say what witness contrary to their own respective faiths is legitimate and must be tolerated, and what constitutes an unfair poaching on neighbors' preserves. But there have been a good many instances of religious bodies appealing to governments to prevent any contradictory witness on the ground that it is proselytism, and an assault upon the integrity of the culture in the given state. Such instances occur usually where there is an established religion, and where the theory of the complete unity of people, culture, church and state prevails.

It will not be easy, especially where there has been theoretical and in practice substantial unity of church and culture, to distinguish between what may be permissible as not overtly contrary to the public order and what the authorities think and feel to be contrary to the general good of the state and its people. Within the next few years, if a strong affirmation by the Vatican Council is generally accepted by church and state authorities in Spain, we shall have doubtless many illustrations of the difficulty of the transfer from the criterion of the public good to that of the public order. And there is currently in Italy the case of a person who is being tried in the courts because he has insulted the Roman Catholic Church. Certainly in some communities in Italy, any insult to Catholics or Catholicism would be likely to disturb the public order.

On the other hand, one can imagine instances where something that a given priest might construe as an insult would really be likely to redound to the public good. Many a progressive bishop's "intervention" on the floor of the Vatican Council would be considered an insult to the church in half the communities of southern Italy. Thus it is clear that the realization of religious liberty depends upon a change of climate not only in the hierarchy but in the community of faith. Many such illustrations could be found also in the history of Protestant communities.

It has been difficult for Protestants to maintain a consistent theory of the separation of church and state. With regard to religious teaching in the public schools, the practice and still the desire of many Protestants is largely a carryover from the days when the national culture was predominantly Protestant, and few could be found to question the propriety of what amounted to Protestant instruction in the public schools. In the field of higher education and in the case of hospitals, Protestants have found excellent reasons for seeking or accepting government aid, and indeed it is possible to adduce some reasonable distinctions between the legitimacy of such a policy for those institutions, and the legitimacy (or illegitimacy) of accepting or seeking tax support for elementary and secondary education involving religious control and curriculum. But the distinctions are hardly compelling and are not too obvious, either for legislators, for the general public, or for Protestants themselves.

Experience may prove that the line is being further blurred by the new Education Act (of which more in the next chapter) and by the Anti-Poverty Program in which, as we have noted, the government is actually inviting religious groups to participate. It would be difficult to find good reasons why they should not participate at community level, but one can see that the task of deciding what is legitimate cooperation between church and state, and what is an unconstitutional violation of the separation of church and state, is not a simple matter, even when self-interest and emotion can be eliminated. These areas of difficult decision served to underscore the importance of the public welfare, the common good, along with legal-constitutional considerations. A report to the June 1965 meeting of the General Board of the National Council of Churches included the following recommendation:

> When instrumentalities created by the Interreligious Committee are corporations which utilize tax funds, they must be social welfare or philanthropic corporations operating in their own right and under their own control for social welfare purposes only. They would not be in the legal category of agents of the sponsoring bodies, though they would enjoy their approbation and recognition, and though they owed their initial origination to church instigation or to the instigation by persons adhering to some church communion or communions.

Mr. Justice Douglas has indicated in more than one of his *dicta* that for him church-state relations have been illegally modified when any financial contribution to a religious program or institution is involved. This would seem to be a rule of easy application in theory, but the experience of legislators in such examples as we have been citing, and shall cite in other chapters, raises the question whether the Justice may not have oversimplified the matter.

On the nature and use of religious liberty, Dr. Littell has observed that it is not an end in itself, "it is to free men for service to truth." Religion and religious liberty, he says, do not demand a doctrinaire dogmatic separation of church and state, for while the political and religious covenants are indeed distinct, the believing citizen is under both covenants. He quotes the church historian of a century ago, Philip Schaff:

> The glory of America is a free Christianity, independent of the secular government, and supported by the voluntary contributions of a free people. This is one of the greatest facts in modern history.

One recalls that James Bryce also found that the American policy which made religious liberty possible and actual was one of the great achievements of the United States.

Dr. Littell continued:

To the extent that we have learned to treasure our differences and our common heritage, religious liberty has acquired a new meaning in the course of our history. It is not toleration. It is not even a necessary, and sometimes reluctant, "fair play" to all concerned. It is dynamic, sustained by voluntary support of religion. It is potential of greater good, based on the dialogue which leads toward a new and finer public consensus. It is above all rooted and grounded in the conviction that if men of good will bring their questions and concerns to the public forum, openly and without deceit, the Lord of history will not fail to provide workable answers from time to time to those whom He has brought thus far along the way.

In his address before the World Congress of the Catholic Press, to which we have referred, Rabbi Gilbert observed:

We Jews, a small people who have outlived mighty kingdoms and celebrated the defeat of countless tyrants, have been preserved by God to this day, so that we might stand in judgment against any and all who think that Power makes Right. Furthermore, our presence in every part of the world, our "exile" as it were, coupled with an insistence on our right to our own integrity as Jews wherever we live, suggests that it might be God's will that men fashion their society in such ways, so that freedom of conscience be guaranteed, religious differences be permitted and civic loyalty be sought only at the highest order of commitment to the public good and not through the imposition of a spiritual uniformity.

Neither Roman Catholic nor Protestant and Orthodox national and world bodies can abandon the concern for religious liberty, nor suddenly become silent about it. They have put their hand to this plow, and were constrained to do so both for the sake of their own liberties and for their self-respect and proper relations with the public. As Professor Hans Küng has said, "Christianity exists for freedom, the freedom of the children of God, freedom in community, freedom (in love) from servitude to sin, freedom for salvation through faith and service" (*The Christian Century,* June 21, 1963). Vatican II had a particular and present responsibility because in Spain and in some countries in Latin America there is a reluctance to allow religious liberty, and any failure on the part of the Council to give support to religious liberty would surely have reinforced the reactionaries in those countries. Also, all the churches must strengthen the hands of Christians behind the various Curtains; in Turkey, where the Eastern Orthodox ecumenical patriarch is kept in constant uneasiness; in India, where Christianity is not universally received with open arms; and in the Moslem countries.

4

CHURCH, STATE, AND EDUCATION

The development of religious liberty and its acceptance is a condition precedent for the solution of many problems of education in a democratic society and for the well-being of that society, but it does not solve them. In this chapter we shall look at two major problems for Americans: What can the public schools do or teach with regard to religion? Who shall pay for religious instruction in non-public schools? We can approach these two problems with a certain security because both public and parochial schools are firmly established in our educational system and have been declared constitutional.

There are besides these two questions some quite important related ones. What are the respective roles in education and religion of the Federal Government, of state governments, and of local governments, or indeed of the community, considered in a sociological and not purely legal sense?

How do we decide where the role of education ceases to predominate and that of welfare should prevail? What are the respective rights of parents and of the society or community? How far may established customs in a given area limit the strict application of legal or constitutional principles: e.g. in the matter of religious observances for graduation exercises and for Christmas and Thanksgiving and other religious or quasi-religious holidays?

Some of the same problems have to be met at college and university level, usually with aspects that differ from those met at the level of elementary and secondary education, where parents' rights and responsibilities play a larger role. The danger of a state monopoly appears to be less in higher education, though some students of the situation think that the use of tax money for grants to private universities means in practice less adequate support for the state institutions of higher learning. Higher education is closely related to the solution of one of the primary problems mentioned above because teachers must be trained in our colleges and universities to distinguish between what can be done and what can't be done in the public schools, and more importantly, to teach fairly and intelligently whatever the community decides ought to be taught and can be taught about religion in the public schools.

Also in the field of higher education, we have to note the responsibility of seminaries. It is from them that we ought to be able to expect the best thinking on the respective roles of church and state and on the necessity and the methods of cooperation between religion and government. Also, as it becomes more and more evident that we shall not really solve our more serious educational problems by debates and majority votes, but only by putting our heads together—Protestants, Catholics, Jews and humanists—we must look to the seminaries for leadership and leaders in a truly ecumenical approach. Further—the seminaries must not only bring the ecumenical movement to bear on education outside the seminaries; they must accept a major responsibility for the development and the propagation of ecumenical understanding, attitudes, and cooperation.

The author is proceeding not only on the assumption but on the firm conviction that what we are pursuing in American education is not an acquiescent uniformity, still less a constrained conformity, but an integrated cultural heritage for each child. The end product will not be the same for each child because what is to be integrated varies with his home background, his racial, religious or national origin, etc. Many of our citizens believe that the public school, limited as it is with regard to religious instruction, cannot be so supplemented by home and church as to integrate the child's culture. They therefore opt for schools whose entire staffs, curriculum and atmosphere are determined by the religious body with which the parents are affiliated. Many Catholics who have exercised or wish to exercise this option are strongly convinced that justice requires that they should not be burdened with the whole cost of these schools. So far, those Lutherans, Anglicans, Adventists and Jews who provide schools under religious auspices for their children have tended to regard their option as purely voluntary and have not sought contributions from tax funds for the support of such schools. The choice by Protestants has been freer than that of others in the sense that, in the period when the public schools were pervaded by a Protestant atmosphere and culture, others might well consider the schools hostile, or at least alien to their needs, while many Protestants merely found them inadequate. So Protestant were the public schools for decades—in curriculum, atmosphere, religious "exercises" and community control—that others felt themselves aliens. Not only was this the case in the author's boyhood; it was true in schools which his sons attended in the South.

The author has long held that a legal-constitutional approach alone would not lead readily to a generally acceptable adjustment of the conflicting views, either as to what the public schools can do about religion, or as to who shall pay for religious instruction given outside the public schools—or for part of the education given in schools organized and controlled by religious bodies. While government, as representative of the whole community, has an inescapable responsibility for education, it does not have the whole responsibility. There is no way by which it can as a legal entity accept and discharge all community responsibility. The community as such, on a semi-legal governmental, semi-voluntary basis can avail itself of the contribution of religious bodies, of the dramatic and musical arts, and of entertainment and recreation facilities. These considerations and some recent experiments and decisions suggest that we may find the solution of our two primary problems, and perhaps most of the subsidiary ones, not by dividing duties and finances between private and public schools, but by a community approach to what would amount to a common school in the small community, and a common school system in a larger one.

One example of an experiment which points in the direction of a common school is Case No. 18 in the Case Series in Educational Administration of the University Council for Educational Administration. This case was reported to an institute sponsored in cooperation with the Project. Neither the public high school nor the parochial high school in "Midville" had enough students to justify the cost of adequate equipment, curriculum or staff. The public school was in danger of losing its charter. The parochial school might have expanded into surrounding territory, but not without complications. Community leaders succeeded in combining the two schools in September 1961. Temporarily at least, the parochial high school building was leased by the public school district. It remained available for parish use after school hours and for religious instruction before the beginning of the common school session each morning. Books in the parochial high school library suitable for general use were purchased by the Board of Education and placed in the common library. Course offerings were expanded from twenty-five to forty-two. Lay teachers from the parochial high school were retained for the common school. Religious ornaments, etc., were removed from the common school walls. (A cross which was part of the masonry of the parochial building remained and was not protested—it was not a crucifix.) Revision and increase of staff meant increased costs; a new levy of 6 mills was voted 642 to 395.

In the discussion of this case in the institute, one speaker said that he detected "a promise of maturity and reason in the processes that we have learned in order to deal with them." That discussant regarded the "Midville" case as "a particular and a typical solution of a religion and education issue" and therefore refused to generalize about its legal or general acceptability. He concluded that

What may be a moral derivative is the process of an American community's working out a dilemma. Those who were most directly affected sought:

1. A sympathetic hearing for their case;
2. Public recognition of their problem and
3. Help in working out an equitable solution.

A second discussant was very favorably impressed by the concomitant learnings of this experiment. Children of the combined high schools became integrated quickly into one student body. The whole community accepted the national belief that there must be freedom of religion and separation of the functions of church and state.

A third discussant blamed "Midville" severely for having drifted into the situation which required such a solution, but agreed that "under all of its circumstances, 'Midville' probably did a fair job of 'solutioning' its problem."

BIBLE READING AND PRAYER

Beginning with 1948 the United States Supreme Court has handed down decisions on appeals in cases which bear for the most part negatively on religious instruction and observances in the public schools. We quote "A Shorthand Review" from a paper by Jefferson D. Fordham delivered at a law institute sponsored by the Project at the University of Chicago Law School, October 1963:

In the first of these cases, *McCollum v. Board of Education,* the Champaign, Illinois, released-time program was found to violate the establishment clause. That was in 1948. Under this program children were given religious instruction on the school premises by outside persons approved by the school authorities during the secular school day. Four years later a New York City released-time program was upheld in *Zorach v. Clauson,* the distinguishing feature being that the religious instruction was given off school premises. We then have the *Engel* case in 1962, in which the required recitation of a prayer, composed by state officials, from which pupils could be excused on request, was held to violate the establishment clause. And this year the practice of reading verses from the Old or New Testament and reciting the Lord's Prayer in public schools, from which children could be excused, on parental request, was also held to violate this provision in the *Schempp* and *Murray* cases from Pennsylvania and Maryland respectively.

Let us look first at the later cases, since they gave rise to proposals for amending the Constitution, the chief of which was the proposed Becker Amendment which Congress refused to approve in 1964. The Reverend Dean Kelley of the National Council of Churches listed in Methodist *Concern* thirteen reasons adduced for the amendment and seventeen against. Among the reasons alleged for such an amendment are: that the Court is aiding minority groups to veto the religious rights of the majority; that it is helping children to conclude that religion is not "respectable" or important; that the professed neutrality results in *de facto* establishment of secular humanism; and that the amendment sought merely to return to the situation prior to the 1962 and 1963 decisions. Those decisions, it is alleged, tend to separate religion from government, yielding not freedom of religion but freedom from religion. Prayers and Bible reading, it is held, strengthen the moral foundations of our society and have an important symbolic value. The trend to the decisions is held to be alarming, presaging the abolition of military chaplains, tax exemptions for houses of worship and the like.

Certain comments seem appropriate before recording the contrary arguments reported by Dean Kelley. "Freedom from religion," as far as it means freedom from coercion, direct or indirect, is a practically inevitable consequence, if one applies the spirit of the First Amendment to the cases under consideration. Even more important: there can be no freedom of conscience, of witness, of

worship which excepts or excludes the freedom of minorities—
however "off-beat" or distasteful to the majority—unless there is
an immediate and serious threat to public peace or order. Roger
Williams and William Penn were distinctly off-beat and distasteful
to the majority of their contemporaries—as were the early Christian martyrs, and the Old Testament prophets before them.

By direct coercion is meant, in these cases, the combination of
compulsory attendance at school with required religious manifestations or exercises that are unacceptable to one or more minorities.
To excuse some children is to subject them to the inexorable and
pitiless coercion of being regarded by their fellow pupils as "different"—as well as to visualize and emphasize to all the children that
religion is a divisive force in the school and in the community.

Arguments against the proposed amendment, as summarized by
Dean Kelley, hold that the decisions do not prohibit the "free
exercise of religion." Any official intervention on behalf of prayers, Scripture and religion in our pluralist society raises the question "Whose?" Common core or nonsectarian prayers have little
religious effectiveness, and their effect may even be negative. Devotional practices in a public school with compulsory attendance
are not really voluntary; the free exercise of religion belongs to
voluntary groups—not to groups compulsorily assembled. School
children are not removed from their normal communities the way
persons in institutions or in the armed forces are. A school under
government auspices cannot properly give religious instruction for
children from nonreligious homes. The nonreligious person is
properly protected by the First Amendment in his freedom *from*
religion. The majority in a given community may fluctuate, and it
may have a different opinion from that of the majority in another
community. Religion is essentially voluntary; historically it has not
been dependent upon the state for its life and growth. Prayer particularly is more likely to lose than to gain in meaning when supported or prescribed by the government, and may well become
merely a show of prayer. Finally, it is rather anomalous that persons support the amendment as defenders of the church and state

when in fact, as Franklin Littell has said, the test and essence of the American experiment in church-state relations is the "separation of the religious Covenant from the civil Covenant."

Reactions against the 1963 decisions were on the whole more thoughtful and less violent than to the 1962 decision in *Engel vs. Vitale*. The NCCJ devoted three issues of its bulletin, *Dialogue,* to these decisions. Many religious leaders and some religious bodies issued statements calling for calm consideration of what the Court had said and had not said. Nevertheless the Republican platform in 1964 included a statement that the party would guarantee:

> Support of a constitutional amendment permitting those individuals and groups who choose to do so to exercise their religion freely in public places, provided religious exercises are not prepared or prescribed by the state or political subdivision thereof and no person's participation there is coerced, thus preserving the traditional separation of church and state.

The reader is invited to experiment with writing such an amendment.

It is important to note what is not prohibited by the Supreme Court decisions. In the combined *Schempp-Murray* decision, the majority opinion (read by Mr. Justice Clark) included these words:

> Nothing we have said here indicates that such study of the Bible, or of religion, when presented objectively as part of a secular program of education, may not be effected consistent with the First Amendment. . . .

The proper line of distinction would seem to be that what is truly and clearly for educational purposes is legally permissible; and anything intended or used for devotional purposes or for sectarian indoctrination comes under the ban of the Supreme Court decisions. A statement issued by a work group at the National Study Conference on Church and State of the National Council of Churches in 1964, not binding on the council, included these words:

> Far from being anti-religious, these decisions offer us a real opportunity to explore in a new way, the relationship of religious values to the *total* program of the public school. . . .
> The Supreme Court took special care to commend a particular constitutional place for teaching *about* religion in public education. Objective teaching about the influence of religion in history and in contemporary society is not restricted. The full dimensions of these patterns of relationship between religion and public education are not yet known, nor will they easily be defined. But we here affirm our own full support of the endeavor and call upon the churches to enter upon this task with anticipation, confidence and vigor.

The way and the invitation seem clear; the schools may not teach religion in the sense of indoctrination, devotion, commitment; they may teach about religion as a vital, important part of the child's culture and a factor in national and world history which cannot be ignored.

There is need and opportunity for widely varied experiments as to what can be taught properly and effectively, at what levels of the pupils' age and learning, by whom, and in what relation to the curriculum. Parents, school boards, administrators and teachers are *all* involved, and must prepare carefully if the experiment is to succeed. There have been experiments in a few places, but these would as a rule need to be evaluated in the light of the 1962-63 Supreme Court decisions and of the 1965 Education Act with its provisions for shared time (see next section). Study of "teaching about religion" by university-related groups representing both religion and education is urgently needed.

It can scarcely be disputed that there are religious elements and references—in history, literature and art—that cannot be ignored or inadequately treated without distorting the curriculum. Religion itself can probably be appropriately studied (not "taught") only on a comparative basis; this is hardly possible and advisable below the level of the eighth or tenth grade.

SOME PERIPHERAL PROBLEMS

Some of the problems in the relation of religion to education are probably more annoying to a few parents and to school administrators than truly significant to the community as a whole. One of these is the problem of releasing children for religious holidays which are not also national holidays. It would be generally agreed that there must be no partiality, no discrimination. In determining which holidays afford adequate justification for excusing children of one faith or one denomination, the school authorities must take into account the extent of the community consensus with regard to religious holidays, and the frequency of such excuses which is consistent with keeping the pupils of different faiths abreast of each other in their class work.

Practices with regard to religious exercises for graduates from high school are varied. Some communities arrange for a minister of the majority faith to preach a sermon. It would seem unwise to require the attendance at such a service by the students of another faith who are graduating. In some communities it is left to the different churches and synagogues to provide a baccalaureate religious service for their own students. Some schools or communities decide to have no religious service that can be considered official for all the graduates. This tendency will probably prevail more and more, with varying practices by the churches and synagogues.

There has been much discussion and some perplexity over the proper place of religious clubs in the high school. If community opinion permits it, there would seem to be no reason why religious clubs might not have the same privileges as clubs for sports, or for literary exercises or political discussion. That is, they might be permitted to meet out of school hours, on school premises, with faculty supervision and with no favoring of one sect or faith over another.

While Protestant ministers have frequently been engaged as public school teachers, there would probably be a Protestant outcry in practically any case where a Catholic nun or priest was engaged to teach in a public school. If and as we approach the ideal of a common school, there would seem to be little reason, if any, for maintaining this somewhat curious distinction. It might well be, however, that priests or sisters, if employed as teachers in a common school (still more if employed in existing public schools), should not wear their religious habits. Some nuns have quite recently been given permission to wear secular clothing for special assignments. As the ecumenical movement matures, it may become less and less true that "the habit makes the priest." One notes that in the case of a merged school cited earlier in this chapter, religious symbols were removed from classrooms which were to be used by students of more than one faith.

There has been much controversy and some litigation over the erection of religious statues or other symbols, particularly the cross, on public property. In one much publicized case a cross was erected on the grounds of a junior high school; its presence there was negative both for religion and for religious peace. Any religious effect that the symbols may have seems likely to be offset by the resulting divisions in a religiously pluralistic community.

There has likewise been much controversy as to the right of public school or municipal authorities to impose vaccination on those who object to it on religious grounds. The authorities are not likely to hesitate if there is convincing evidence that an epidemic is in progress or imminent. Where a single person is involved, the case is somewhat different: e.g., when a blood transfusion or an amputation is required by the medical profession in order to save a life. Similar questions arise in the matter of continued administration of drugs to keep a patient alive when there is no medical prognosis of possible recovery. Again the rights and safety of a community would seem to have moral precedence over those of an individual. But by the same token, extreme care should be taken to arrive at something like a consensus involving, e.g., several competent physicians independent of each other, with perhaps the addition of representatives of the religious and other elements in the community.

For several paragraphs we seem to have been rather more in the process of cataloguing problems than of solving them or discussing them adequately. They have in common, to justify at least a brief reference, an obvious susceptibility to an ecumenical approach by the community, each group, religious and secular, seeking consensus rather than victory. Some of these cases may at least occasionally afford examples of situations where religious liberty must yield, not to the immediate requirements of public order, but to those of the public good—as judged by the community.

Before we look at a proposed partial solution for both the curriculum and the financial problems, we must look at the other major question proposed at the outset of this chapter: how to finance religious education outside the public school.

CONSTITUTIONAL GUIDELINES ON
FINANCING RELIGIOUS INSTRUCTION

At a Project-sponsored institute at the University of Chicago Law School, October 1963, Prof. Harry W. Jones of Columbia University proposed eight theses related to interpreting Supreme Court decisions—they might be helpful also in forecasting them. We reproduce some of them in approximate summary: It is difficult to separate law from policy, judicial from legislative responsibility; the "framers'" intention, the understanding on the part of their contemporaries, State Court decisions—these are instructive but not controlling; a distinction, at least in policy, can be made between aid to elementary and that to higher education, in private schools. Dr. Jones propounded a hypothetical case to illustrate the freedom and the difficulty of the Supreme Court.

In case federal funds were to be made available by statute, directly or through the states, for free standard textbooks, free lunches, bus transportation, certain school health services, foreign languages, and laboratory facilities for physics and chemistry in schools private and public, Dr. Jones sees three arguable stages of permissiveness on the part of the Supreme Court: (1) the statute is constitutional (if there is no discrimination among or on behalf of church-related schools); (2) aid to the pupil is justified for four of the items, but the decision on languages and laboratories might go either way; (3) the whole statute might be held unconstitutional as a violation of the Establishment Clause. The Court, Dr. Jones held, "could legitimately decide the case on any one of the three theories suggested and justify its result in full accordance with all the proprieties of our legal system." (We note that the New Jersey Everson Case on bus transportation and an earlier Louisiana textbook case involved state, not federal, funds.)

BUS TRANSPORTATION

Among the so-called fringe benefits for parochial schools or their pupils, bus transportation is probably the most controverted and litigated. The supplying out of state tax funds of such textbooks as may be used in public schools has been held to be not contrary to the United States Constitution. (The Cochran Case, 1929, appealed from Louisiana.) Lunches and health services available to public schools may also be made available to parochial schools.

The important Supreme Court decision on bus transportation is the Everson Case, February 1947. This held that a New Jersey statute allowing a district school board to provide transportation to and from schools, some of which are not public schools, was not contrary to the Federal Constitution. This was a 5 to 4 decision, and Mr. Justice Rutledge protested vigorously that the majority decision represented a regrettable departure from the principle of the separation of church and state. The Supreme Court decision did not touch on the question whether the federal government might give such aid for bus transportation. This decision seems to have been based quite clearly on the "child benefit" theory.

Any statute providing for bus transportation for parochial school pupils has to face the constitutional question in the state where it is proposed. The state constitution has in many cases been held to prohibit such aid.

In some cases bus transportation for non-public-school pupils is limited as to distance or to the route used for the public schools. In some rural areas the cost of transportation amounts to a very large proportion of the school budget.

In a background report of NCCJ, January 1963, Dr. Theodore Powell describes the process used at Wilton, Connecticut, to determine whether public bus transportation should be provided for parochial school students. The 1957 General Assembly had provided that towns which did not provide such service might decide their policy by local referendum. After considerable discussion both public and private, 44% of the electorate voted and the proposal was defeated 1189 to 750. Later a committee of parents proposed that Catholic school pupils be permitted to ride the public school busses, and that the parents pay a proportionate share of the cost. The school board agreed. Many, both Protestant and Catholic, regretted the adverse vote in the referendum, and renewed their efforts to bring about better communication between Protestants and Catholics in the community.

DIRECT AID TO PAROCHIAL SCHOOLS

While much language can be found in Supreme Court opinions to the effect that tax support for non-public schools would be in violation of the First Amendment, there is respectable legal opinion on the other side. At the Project's Atlanta Institute on Public Education and Religion, October 1964, Prof. Wilber Katz cited the opinion of himself and two Harvard professors of constitutional law in hearings before a Senate education subcommittee "that the First Amendment does not forbid non-discriminatory aid to all schools for costs of education in secular subjects." This opinion was supported by Prof. Marion Rice of the University of Georgia in the Atlanta Institute: "National aid to secular education in the parochial schools is a legitimate exercise of the national power."

There is much Catholic support for outright and direct aid to the private school as such. In the 1962 Project meetings in New York Mr. Donald Gill, then of the National Association of Evangelicals, said, "It is not the function of the public to provide national support for church schools which are not under public control." Rev. John Reedy, Editor of *Ave Maria,* replied, "In my judgment such answers on the political level will hardly satisfy the Catholic parent who must budget for his six children attending the parochial school. Reasonable as it may appear, they will not satisfy the financial burden of a Catholic parent who is convinced that his rights to educate his children will be jeopardized if such public funds are not made available for parochial school education. Furthermore he is convinced that his educational system serves the public weal by educating children for citizenship and through this very program of relating secular education to spiritual and moral ideas."

Dr. David LaDriere of Citizens for Educational Freedom added this comment: "Why cannot we apply to public education the procedures we have already adopted at the level of the university? For example, at the university level there is the G.I. Bill and there are forty-one programs of government that provide for higher education without discrimination against schools under church auspices."

Speakers in other institutes have held that the parallel between higher education and elementary and secondary education is not convincing. We may note that no such weakening of public education from the G.I. Bill or other present governmental subsidies to colleges and universities is likely, as would almost certainly occur at elementary and secondary level if every religious denomination were encouraged to seek tax support even indirectly for its schools. The danger of such confusion is minimized by some Catholics, partly because there are already more than five million children in Catholic parochial schools, and it would require, they say, much more than a presumably small subsidy from government to induce other religious bodies to launch a parochial school program. But there are considerable numbers already enrolled in Protestant and Jewish schools with religious support. There would surely be great resistance among many others over the thought of paying from tax funds for education in a religion other than their own. Some Protestants ask why, if religious instruction in parochial schools is aided from tax funds, Sabbath schools and released-time instruction should not be supported from the same source.

For all alike there is the question whether government financing can be had without government control. It is perhaps partly for this reason that one can cite from various Catholic bishops in recent years statements against federal aid to education, coupled however with the strong assertion that Catholic parents, compelled by law to educate their children and sending them on grounds of conscience to church-related schools, should be aided by the government.

One notes that there is a theoretical and possibly a legal distinction between "aid to all schools for costs of education in secular subjects" and aid to parochial schools as such. The same is true of aid to parents of children attending parochial schools. In practice, payments to parents may be made to aid the parochial school, whose primary purpose is the aid of religion—Protestant, Jewish, Catholic, Orthodox, Moslem, Buddhist. Aid for secular subjects may mean the margin between maintaining and closing the school, or between not organizing a parochial school in a community and organizing one. Financial aid to parents could mean higher tuition payments, reducing the church's financial burden.

It may be that with fringe benefits and with experiments in shared time, Catholics as a whole will not for a time push very hard for direct aid to parochial schools. They and the nation as a whole may prefer to experiment for a few years and see whether the child-benefit theory can be accepted as a practical compromise between strict separation and government aid to religion.

The Vatican Council's language, in section 5 of its Declaration on Christian Education, seems to allow for different methods and degrees of subsidizing religious education:

> Parents who have the primary and inalienable right and duty to educate their children must enjoy true liberty in their choice of schools. Consequently, the public power, which has the obligation to protect and defend the rights of citizens, must see to it, in its concern for distributive justice, that public subsidies are paid out in such a way that parents are truly free to choose according to their conscience the schools they want for their children.

In different institutes of the NCCJ Project, Prof. George La Noue and Dr. Theodore Powell have laid down and defended guidelines to govern federal aid (government aid in general) to elementary and secondary education. Most of the substance of those guidelines is also included in a "Resolution on Federal Aid to Education" adopted by the General Board of the National Council of Churches February 26, 1965:

> 1. That benefits intended for all children be determined and administered directly by public agencies responsible to the electorate (whether directly or indirectly);

> 2. That such benefits intended for all children not be conveyed in such a way that religious institutions acquire property or the services of personnel thereby;

> 3. That such benefits not be used directly or indirectly for the inculcation of religion or the teaching of sectarian doctrine; and

4. That there be no discrimination by race, religion, class, or national origin in the distribution of such benefits.

Since these distinctions are subtle, and the principles at stake important, adequate provision for judicial review should be included in any legislation on this subject.

These guidelines seem also rather closely consistent with the Act of Congress signed by President Johnson on April 10, 1965.

RELEASED TIME AND SHARED TIME

For many years in many places students have been released from public school classes in order to attend classes in religious instruction. This permits, indeed it necessitates, a schedule of staggered releases. One variant is to shorten the school day so that all students are released at the same time to go or not to go for religious instruction elsewhere. If all students intended to take advantage of this dismissal for purposes of religious instruction, "dismissed time" would have obvious advantages over released time both on constitutional grounds and for administrative reasons. In the pattern usually followed in released time, pupils are actually released on the basis of their attendance of classes of religious instruction. Since this is done at the request of the parents, attendance could be left to the responsibility of the parents, relieving school authorities from applying truancy regulations (unless intolerable abuses should develop). In the McCollum and Zorach cases mentioned by Jefferson D. Fordham above, the United States Supreme Court helped to determine some limits for released-time practices:

The Court decided, in the McCollum Case, that the Champaign (Illinois) system of released-time religious instruction, in school buildings, during school hours, under teachers provided for sectarian groups by their respective authorities, with administrative cooperation and (undefined) supervision by public school authorities, was unconstitutional. As some of the Justices pointed out, this decision did not make clear what the Court would decide in another released-time situation wherein one or more elements were different. But the language of the ruling opinion seemed to invalidate widespread practices under released-time arrangements regardless of where the classes for religious instruction might be held.

In 1952, nevertheless, six Justices magnified the importance of the fact that in the Zorach Case, appealed from New York, released-time classes met outside the public school buildings, and upheld the New York practice. Dissenting Justices considered the majority ruling a reversal of McCollum; and Justice Jackson characterized the distinction "trivial, almost to the point of cynicism." A distinction apparently more vital was that the majority found no evidence of compulsion in the record before the Court; the dissenters did. The majority were unwilling to uphold a doctrine of rigid and absolute separation, saying in fact: "When the State encourages religious instruction or cooperates with religious authorities by adjusting the schedule of public events to sectarian needs, it follows the best of our traditions."

(Claud Nelson, *Church and State*)

Released time has demonstrated its usefulness, but its use is still limited. If its use were greatly extended, there would presumably be less demand for full-curriculum non-residential schools under religious auspices. The fact is, however, that several million children of all three major religious groups are in full-curriculum schools under religious auspices. Assuming that both public and private schools maintain proper educational standards, this should raise primarily the question of needless and expensive duplication of equipment and curriculum courses. There would thus be ample ground for considering the possibilities of shared time, even if there were no competition whatever between public and private schools for tax funds. In fact, however, much of the discussion of shared time or dual enrollment takes place in the financial area. Although there had been many earlier isolated and partial instances of its use, the discussion has become meaningful in the sense of seeming to present a live and general option only since 1960.

From NCCJ's *Dialogue* bulletin on shared time (June 1964) we quote excerpts from an earlier *Look* article by Louis Cassels:

> On November 22, 1960, about forty Protestant and Catholic officials met privately at the Hotel Woodner in Washington, D.C., to discuss topics of common concern, including the question of religious exercises in public schools and the controversy over aid to parochial schools. Toward the end of a long day, in which each side had restated its own views and no agreement seemed in sight, Dr. Stearns suggested shared time as a step in the right direction.
>
> The idea struck sparks. Both groups decided that it was worth further investigation, and they agreed to convene another private meeting, with Jewish leaders and public-school officials participating. The second meeting was held at the Interchurch Center in New York on October 11, 1961. Some of those present had serious doubts about shared time, but the consensus of the meeting was expressed by Rabbi Arthur Gilbert of New York: "It is worth a try."

Rev. Dean M. Kelley wrote in the Methodist *Christian Advocate:*

> "Shared time" is a plan first suggested by Protestants. Erwin Shaver, Theodore Powell, John C. Bennett, Claud Nelson and others had outlined this plan in one form or another. But it remained for a Presbyterian public-school superintendent, Harry Stearns, to outline the plan in detail

and propose it in educational circles. [See reference to Religious Education Symposium below.]

. . . "Shared time" is based on the assumption that all the children in the community have the right to attend the public school, but that they need not make an all-or-nothing choice between public and private schools.

There is no reason why private school systems should need to construct expensive laboratories, gyms, or vocational shops duplicating those in the public schools if the children who attend parochial schools could take these subjects in public schools.

Much has been written in the past five years for and against shared time. Important experiments are going forward in various areas. While there are lawyers who consider shared time unconstitutional, and while the American Civil Liberties Union has declared its opposition to the plan (April 1965), there seems to be so far no adverse court decision and there are many at least semi-official opinions supporting its constitutionality.

A recent survey indicated that both private and public school administrators who had been involved in shared-time projects favored their continuance. There are of course administrative problems to be solved, and there is potentially a great problem of transportation from one school to the other. In Chicago a pilot project is being planned in which the new Catholic high school will be built adjacent to a public high school with which it will cooperate.

The Central Conference of American Rabbis (CCAR) in 1964 adopted this statement:

. . . While we have the highest regard for proponents of the plan who see in it a means of promoting inter-religious dialogue, we seriously question the wisdom of shared time. It may accentuate religious differences; it may involve religious functionaries in various aspects of public school administration, curriculum planning and scheduling; it may result in derogating from the importance of the public school by assigning to it less important subjects, while imposing on it greater administrative burdens; and it may encourage a proliferation of sectarian school systems.

The CCAR report, recognizing ongoing "experiments," set forth certain "guidelines or caveats" which, it felt, should be followed in order to preserve the nonsectarian character of the program in the public schools.

On the other hand, the National Council of Churches said in a policy statement of June 1964:

The rapidly increasing number of children and the rapidly increasing costs of education, along with other factors, have caused Roman Catholic educators and parents in recent years to ask for public funds in discharging part or all of their educational responsibility. Assistance is often asked for that portion of the task most clearly identified with "general education." Protestants and Orthodox educators and others have generally not favored the use of tax funds for church-related schools.

So far this unresolved difference has prevented direct grants to religious elementary and secondary schools; it has also hindered the passage of general legislation for federal aid to public education.

We know of no legal opinion[1] holding that dual school enrollment violates the federal constitution. Most states' constitutions or educational legislation appear to permit or not forbid dual school enrollment.

[1] (An intended substitution of "judicial decision" for "legal opinion" was inadvertently overlooked.)

We therefore approve further experimentation with, and continuing evaluation of dual school enrollment for classroom instruction as a viable provision for those who, for conscience sake, maintain separate schools.

The 1965 Education Act includes provision for the use of shared time in certain circumstances and on a limited scale; thus both the administrative and legislative branches of the Federal Government hold it to be constitutional.

At the first national meeting held by the Project in New York in May 1962, one of the topics was Religion and Education. Msgr. John B. McDowell, Superintendent of Pittsburgh Catholic Schools, proposed more than one hundred questions. While he did not propose them as a disinterested bystander, they were honest questions, well illustrating the tremendous range and complexity of the subject. It is not without significance, therefore, that Msgr. McDowell has been active in the promotion and administration of one of the most interesting and successful experiments in shared time.

Among the questions proposed, as was inevitable, were those concerning the rights of parents with regard to the education of their children. Without piling up material on this subject, one may perhaps suggest that the parents' rights and responsibilities are related to and limited by those of other parents, and thus by the interest of the total community. Also, one must not overlook the fact that parents' notions as to what is proper and adequate education for the child may be quite inadequate and antisocial in themselves, and may at some point come into conflict with the child's notions. The child's notions, if he has been generally well-instructed and alert up to junior high school level, may sometimes be sounder than those of his parents. In brief, the parents' rights, while primary, are not absolute or exclusive.

In a recent study, *God in Education,* Dr. Niels C. Nielsen, Jr., comes to this conclusion: "The shared-time program is assuredly one of the most creative proposals yet offered to help solve the public-parochial school dilemma."

THE ELEMENTARY AND SECONDARY
EDUCATION ACT OF 1965

We quote from the April 1965 issue of *American Education* put
out by the United States Department of Health, Education and
Welfare:

Education history was written this month when President
Johnson signed into law the Elementary and Secondary Education Act of 1965.

The purpose of the new law, which authorizes more than
$1,300,000,000 in Federal funds to be channelled into the
Nation's classrooms, is to:
   · Strengthen elementary and secondary school programs
for educationally deprived children in low income areas.
   · Provide additional school library resources, textbooks,
and other instructional materials.
   · Finance supplementary educational centers and services.
   · Broaden areas of cooperative research.
   · Strengthen State departments of education.

The Act is widely hailed as a breakthrough, at last, for federal
aid to education. Such aid was long blocked because upholders of
church-state separation would not permit the adoption of provisions for financial aid to religiously-controlled schools, and the
supporters, especially Catholics, of such schools would not support
federal aid to education unless these schools were to benefit from it
directly. The Act may be interpreted, therefore, as a compromise,
increasing indirect aid to parochial schools, relieving their burdens
through supplementary services, especially to underprivileged children, through dual enrollment, through general aid to educational
research and to school libraries. Books and equipment made available to private schools will be under loan. If damaged or worn out,
they would be replaced by the borrower; in many cases the loans

will be for a specified period, and definitely returnable to the government authorities which retain title throughout. The editor of the journal of the teachers' fraternity, *Phi Delta Kappan* (May 1965) roundly denounces the retention of title as a subterfuge and foresees that historians a quarter century hence will look on the passage of this Act, not so much as a breakthrough for federal aid, but as a body blow to church-state separation. He points out that since Roman Catholics have more children than others in parochial schools, they will be major beneficiaries. There are many Protestants who wonder whether the price paid for a beginning in federal aid may not be excessive.

The Act would seem indubitably to rest at many points on an expanded application of the "child benefit" theory. Two Southern educators in the same issue of *Phi Delta Kappan* oppose that theory itself, maintaining that pupils and school form an identity and cannot be separated. Certain provisions of the Act will be challenged in the courts as to their constitutionality. Since the National Education Association, the National Catholic Welfare Conference and the National Council of Churches have all given direct or indirect support to the Bill which has now become the Act, one may expect that the Supreme Court will hesitate long before outlawing the measure on grounds of public policy, and that it will not regard those provisions which rest upon the "child benefit" theory as an undue expansion of its application, provided state and private school authorities apply it in good faith, and in sincere and effective cooperation.

It is difficult to find in the Act cause for alarm as to the extension of federal control of education. Obviously there will be some indirect effects of that nature, but one may well feel more uneasiness as to the possibility that state educational authorities might find occasions for undue extension of their authority and control, both over public and private local school authorities.

The New York Times editorially finds it a gain in our pluralist society that under dual enrollment many parochial school children would be enrolled in public schools for some of their instruction. It is important that care be taken that these pupils come in as individuals, not as classes dismissed from private schools. If dual enrollment should be extensively used, we might begin to see a sort of reversal in the process of integrating the pupil's general culture and his religious culture. The task of the religiously controlled school is to integrate the general culture into the religious. If now the process becomes one of integrating the religious culture into a general culture which is actually shared by Protestants, Jews and Catholics, we may indeed move in the direction of a pluralistic society rather than an aggregation of sharply differentiated religious cultures, and this with no sacrifice for the adherent of any faith.

Worthy of note is the close relation of the Education Act to the Anti-Poverty Program. Of the $967 million already appropriated for school assistance, over $767 million "will go to public school districts that have substantial numbers of low-income students. . . . While the funds go only to the public schools, the special programs and services created with the Federal money would be available to students in parochial and other private schools . . . [They] are to share, too, in other Federally aided programs created under the new law." (*The New York Times,* January 12, 1966).

One must note also that parochial schools cannot long remain static: they will be profoundly affected by the new Catholicism—and catholicity—recognized and fostered by the Vatican Council. Any symbolism or propagation of a defensive or ghetto mentality (which has sometimes been evident) will have to yield.

At the least, we may conclude, we are no longer at an impasse in the financing of education or in religious instruction. Released time, dual enrollment, and "child benefit" offer ways around or out of our controversies. These should be fully tested by communities and by the nation in the ecumenical spirit and hope. Even partial solutions here will substantially reduce the roadblocks on the way to the great society.

5

ADDITIONAL ISSUES
INVOLVING BOTH RELIGION
AND GOVERNMENT

Open and controverted questions on tax exemption for church property, military chaplains, conscientious objectors to some or all military service, and diplomatic relations with a church may be regarded either as issues of principle between church and state, or as practical problems involving both religion and government. Some of them overlap the zone of law and morality issues where, however, prohibition, censorship, Sunday closing laws, divorce, birth control, and capital punishment more clearly belong. The same is true of open-occupancy housing measures, to be noted under race relations. "Right-to-work" laws are on the fringe of church-state relations with an area of definite overlap. All these problems have in common at least two characteristics: one, that they are open and controverted; two, that a united approach to them on the part of the religious forces of the nation would greatly aid in achieving socially beneficial solutions.

TAX EXEMPTION

Although exemption from taxes for the property of religious organizations constitutes an undeniable subsidy to religion, defenders of the separation of church and state do not usually think of tax exemption as a violation of the principle. They would tend, rather, especially in view of the long-practiced extension and enjoyment of this privilege, to think of its repeal as an extension of the authority of government over religion. Neither does there seem to be any great objection or questioning regarding tax exemption, either by those not religiously affiliated or by government authorities, as long as it extends only to property used for worship, for religious instruction or for charitable purposes—other charitable organizations also enjoy tax exemption.

There is some question as to tax exemption for living quarters for pastors, and much more with regard to income-producing facilities, even if all the income above expenses is plowed back into definitely religious activities. Some years ago tax exemption for Y.M.C.A. hotels was challenged by the management of hotels with which they competed, and the Y.M.C.A. as a result confines its dormitory patronage to members—though it is possible for the term of membership to be limited to the period of residence. Among income-producing facilities enjoying tax exemption for some time were the production of wine, in one case, and bread in another by Roman Catholic orders. The courts have removed the tax exemption in the case of the wine.

Some Protestant churchmen have become uneasy with regard to tax exemption for large and powerful denominations. This is partly because they feel that religious institutions already enjoy many economic benefits from the community and ought to contribute to community expenses rather than add to their own financial reserves. There have been a few recent examples of voluntary contributions by local churches to municipal budgets.

But more frightening than the annual loss to government is the accumulation of properties acquired because of tax exemption, or in some cases by government grant, which go on increasing in value, without corresponding effort or service on the part of the religious bodies that own them. In medieval times this was known as the power of the "dead hand." The phenomenon has by no means disappeared in this country or abroad. In Russia at the time of the First World War, it was said that the income from the urban property of one Protestant denomination was sufficient to finance its entire work in Russia. The author witnessed an example of the benefit to the Y.M.C.A. of land appreciation in a European city. It is evident that good faith on the part of religious authorities, and vigilance on the part of the citizens, are in order. If, for example, a church is wisely holding property which it is sure to need for its own future use, there might well be a moderate tax levy, with an additional payment in case the land were sold for non-church use. It is possible for religious bodies to hold enough land exempt in an urban area to constitute a serious burden for taxpayers, and to raise the cost of real estate, which means a burden for owners and users of both business and residence property.

One sometimes hears tax exemption defended on the ground that the power to tax is the power to destroy. While this is true in general, and might well apply to church property, it probably is not true of religion itself. The possibility of using taxation in the United States in order to embarrass religious bodies would seem to be so remote as to be negligible. Both here and abroad it also seems practically certain that if a government or a society set out to destroy the churches, it would seek quicker and surer methods than taxing them to death.

MILITARY CHAPLAINS

There is general agreement that soldiers separated from their families and communities and from their churches or synagogues should have available spiritual advisers who can also conduct worship services and perform other ministries of religion. The question, therefore, is whether chaplains should be appointed and paid by the government or by the respective religious bodies. On principle, one might well choose the second alternative. So far, however, the practical objections have seemed insuperable. But the very fact of being a commissioned officer in the armed forces is almost certain to create a barrier between the chaplain and many of his flock. It may increase the burden on his conscience of trying to contribute to military efficiency, and at the same time serve the interests of peace, which is implicit if not explicit in the commission from the religious body of which he is a minister. Since this conflict of conscience may at times burden some of the men whom he serves, it is important that he himself should have at least faced the problem, and should be able to face it together with those he serves if neither he nor they find it possible to escape the burden.

It seems fair to add that pacifist propaganda in the armed forces in time of war could hardly be tolerated—and would not be. Also, since a chaplain must have some military privileges, e.g., access to men in combat zones, he cannot expect to be exempted from some degree of military discipline.

CONSCIENTIOUS OBJECTORS

Not many countries, if any, are more careful than the United States to recognize and protect the rights of those who conscientiously object to military service. They are permitted to register and apply for alternate service in specified categories, in war or in peace. Many accept noncombatant auxiliary military service, e.g., in the ambulance corps. The test of conscientious objection had until the spring of 1965 included the affirmation of belief in a Supreme Being. Selective Service and the courts have tended toward an elastic interpretation of the requirement. Some draft boards, trying to fill their quotas, have been stricter, giving occasion for many appeals. The Supreme Court has now made it easier for a draft board to recognize "conscience."

It was not until after a number of denials by the Supreme Court—e.g., in the Macintosh case—that conscientious objectors were finally made eligible by the Court to become naturalized citizens of the United States.

Some conscientious objectors refuse to register or to cooperate in any way with the machinery of national defense. Some of them, especially during the world wars, have served prison sentences. This is not necessarily inhuman punishment. The great injustice lies in the fact that their conscience has not been given due respect. They have been treated as felons and permanently deprived of citizenship, and their children are stigmatized.

In France, one who refused military service could until 1964 be imprisoned for the term for which he had been called—not just once, but term after term as long as he was of military age. The remedial legislation is not retroactive.

In Italy, in February 1965, the Tuscany group of retired or reserve military chaplains (with one-sixth of the members present) resolved that they considered "an insult to their country [Patria] and to its fallen, the so-called 'conscientious objection' which, extraneous to the Christian commandment of love, is an expression of cowardice." An isolated country priest, Don Lorenzo Milani, wrote an open letter of over two thousand words, saying that the chaplains should be slow to insult men who obey conscience: "Perhaps tomorrow you will discover that they are prophets. Certainly the place of the prophets is in prison, but it is not good to stand on the side of those who keep them there." In October he defended himself eloquently in 7,000 words to the court, against a charge of criminal libel. He also refuted any imputation of anarchy: "He who pays with his person testifies that he wants the law better, that is, that he loves the law more than others." (*Il Ponte,* 10th issue, 1965) Early in 1966 the court ruled that neither Don Milani nor his publisher had committed any crime.

The Vatican Council's statement on conscientious objection should be of help both in France and Italy, with their Catholic traditions. The third paragraph of division 79 of the *Constitution on the Church in the Modern World* mentions several ways of reducing "the frightfulness of war" and concludes: "Moreover, it seems right that laws make provisions for the case of those who for reasons of conscience refuse to bear arms, provided, however, that they agree to serve the human community in some other way."

"RIGHT TO WORK" LAWS

In 1965, Congress was involved in strenuous and sometimes bitter discussion over the repeal of Section 14B of the Taft-Hartley Law but did not come to a decisive vote. That section has enabled many states to pass or retain laws which are said to make it difficult, if not impossible, for trade unions to enroll all the workers in a plant. Workers and political leaders and churchmen, and possibly those engaged in management, are divided in their convictions with regard to these so-called "right-to-work" laws. There seems to be at this juncture more support by church organizations for repealing than for maintaining Section 14B. It is no easy matter to guarantee the workers' right to organize and bargain, which has been in this country and in Western Europe one of the chief instruments in raising the standard of living and the status of workers, without giving the unions too much power over their members, and in society in general. This is not a matter of religious liberty as such.

Religious liberty is involved, however, in the case of those who conscientiously object to joining unions and submitting themselves to a majority vote of persons who do not share their religious convictions and their attitude toward life. Some conscientious objectors of this particular type are grateful for the services on their behalf which the unions perform and are willing to pay dues even though they do not wish to become members, and thus would have no vote in determining union policy.

The Second Vatican Council, true to the sense of the three great social encyclicals—*Rerum Novarum, Quadragesimo Anno,* and *Mater et Magistra*—sustained both the right to join unions and the right to strike, but in language not decisive as to "right-to-work" laws:

Among the basic rights of the human person is to be numbered the right of freely founding unions for working people. These should be able truly to represent them and to contribute to the organizing of economic life in the right way. Included is the right of freely taking part in the activity of these unions without risk of reprisal. . . . When, however, socio-economic disputes arise, efforts must be made to come to a peaceful settlement. Although recourse must always be had first to a sincere dialogue between the parties, a strike, nevertheless, can remain even in present-day circumstances a necessary, though ultimate, aid for the defense of the workers' own rights and the fulfilment of their just desires. As soon as possible, however, ways should be sought to resume negotiation and the discussion of reconciliation. (Excerpts from division 68, *The Church in the Modern World*)

DIPLOMATIC RELATIONS WITH A CHURCH

The United States maintained a legation to the Papal States from 1848 to 1868. Our minister was instructed by the Secretary of State that his duties did not include any mission to the Pope as head of the Church. When it became evident that the Papal States were likely to be absorbed into a united Italy, Congress deleted the legation to the Papal States from the list of appropriations for diplomatic establishments and thus brought about its termination. To send an ambassador to the Holy See now would not be a resumption of former diplomatic relations. Our legation of a century ago to the secular government of the Papal States has its successor in our embassy to the government of Italy.

Official missions to the Vatican have been sent, very infrequently, when there was a particular issue of importance to be negotiated; e.g., William Howard Taft was sent to confer on an issue that arose in what were then our Philippine Islands territories. Presidents Roosevelt and Truman sent the Honorable Myron Taylor as a personal representative to the Pope. Vatican authorities listed this representation as if it had been an embassy of the United States. In 1951 President Truman nominated General Mark Clark to be an ambassador to the Vatican. Opposition was so vigorous and voluminous that General Clark asked that the nomination be withdrawn, and President Truman decided to drop the matter. Voices have been raised occasionally in the intervening years calling for representation at the Vatican. As late as April 1965 James Reston of *The New York Times* revived the proposal in a column written from Rome.

Commenting on the Reston column, Father John B. Sheerin, C.S.P., in his column, "Sum and Substance," said, "Just when we hoped that the controversy over Vatican-United States diplomatic relations had been forgotten, James Reston stirs up the embers once again . . . why stir up the old witches' cauldron? We are making ecumenical progress and Catholic-Protestant relations were never so good." Father Sheerin held that our government could tap existing sources of information at the Vatican through private emissaries, remarking that he had talked in Rome during the Vatican Council session with a private representative of President Johnson, who had come to Rome on such an errand. Father Sheerin continued, "We don't need the prestige and certainly not the bad impression that diplomatic ties would create." He thinks Mr. Reston would find "that many American bishops who attended the Council are not happy about Catholic involvement in American diplomacy, national or international." Father Sheerin cites voices of bishops in the Council protesting against the Vatican's imitation of the diplomatic institutions of secular powers and concludes, "My guess is that the Council, in striving for evangelical simplicity, has made secular pomp and power more undesirable than ever in the Catholic Church." An editorial of similar purport appeared on June 25, 1965, in *The Oklahoma Courier,* a diocesan paper.

The National Council of Churches was able in 1951-52 to eliminate ninety-nine percent of anti-Catholic animus from its public and private efforts to prevent the Mark Clark appointment. This was not easy then and would not be easy now if a serious effort were made to send an ambassador to the Vatican. There is no need for this issue to be or to become a controversy between two bodies of Christians; it is a test case in church-state relations. The United States has worked out something highly useful and almost unique in those relations. Many citizens, Catholic and non-Catholic, would need to be convinced that there are new and compelling circumstances indicating the need to breach present arrangements, especially if it almost inevitably involved stirring up an artificial but highly emotional religious controversy.

Competent Catholic authorities (e.g., the late Anne O'Hare Mc-Cormick and Father Robert Graham, S.J.) have made it perfectly clear that an ambassador to the Holy See is accredited to the church and not to a state as such. The State of Vatican City established in 1929 has no significance or even existence apart from the Catholic Church. Its inhabitants retain the citizenship of their home country in addition to temporary State of Vatican City citizenship. The author, living in Rome for all or part of fourteen years since 1929, has crossed the Tiber into Vatican City innumerable times without any sense of crossing a frontier, entering or leaving: Vatican City is entirely surrounded by Rome. Furthermore, the suggested parallel with the sending of an ambassador to England, where the Queen is titular head of the established church, has no substance: England would still be a nation and the Queen would still be the Queen if the Church of England were disestablished.

It seemed entirely appropriate for Ambassador Goldberg, at the beginning of 1966, to visit Pope Paul—not as a temporal sovereign but as a head of a church who had sought to enlist the widest possible religious influence on the side of peace.

Why is it thought that the United States should send an ambassador to the Holy See, departing from a tradition that has served the country well, not least the minority religious groups? The burden of proof is certainly on those who propose the innovation. Other nations are represented there, we are told. But they do not have our church-state relations, nor our religious liberty. Also, the European nations had diplomatic relations with the Papal States; not having made the distinction between Papal States and Papacy that the United States had been careful to make, withdrawal of their embassies or legations at the moment of the Papacy's humiliation (its eventual salvation!) would have been most awkward.

Those same Papal States have left a sorry legacy of involvement of the Papacy in Italian politics. In France, the church's political responsibilities are now largely left to the bishops. A similar devolution seems inevitable in Italy, but it has scarcely begun, if at all. Until it is complete, and until the Catholic Church has recovered both from the scandal and the nostalgia of temporal power, why should the United States break a good tradition to give new vigor to a bad one, and depart from sound and clear principles of church-state relations to encourage an unsound and confused pattern?

It is possible that there was an advantage for our nation, when Italy was hostile or divided during the 1940's, in having in Rome a representative of ambassadorial rank; that would be no index to the normal situation. It is claimed that useful information is to be had through a Vatican embassy that is not otherwise obtainable. Would this come through other ambassadors, from countries whose diplomats meet ours in a hundred capitals around the world? The likelihood is less than one percent! Would it come through ecclesiastical channels? Where does the Holy See have more and better observers and reporters than the United States and nations friendly to it? We do not want missionaries to be or to be classed as spies, whether they are Catholic or Protestant.

It is also claimed that representation at the Vatican would strengthen us in our efforts against Communism. But the real fight is against dictatorship: we could make peace with Communist democracies. When democratic Catholics and Protestants can forget the Vatican support for Mussolini, Franco and Salazar in Catholic countries, we can begin to speculate on the prospects of effective political help against Communist dictators and dictatorships. The Vatican has long been willing to receive an ambassador from Russia: would that strengthen the Kremlin in its fight against democracy?

Whenever our government needs to ask questions of Catholics, or seek accommodations with them, to whom could it address itself with greater propriety than to the bishops of the United States? This would make practical use of collegiality, and perhaps stimulate similar decentralization in other parts of the world. Since any effective communication will eventually involve the American hierarchy, conversation via Rome seems needlessly awkward. Actually, the recent popes and the Vatican Council have been moving away from the show and trappings of the Holy See's diplomatic corps, recognizing that Christianity's impact for human betterment does not depend on having papal nuncios as deans of diplomats in the nations' capitals, but on doing well those things that pertain to the church's vocation. Americans can and do assist all the churches and synagogues in myriad ways that do not depend on diplomatic relations with a church. Let the church *be* the church!

SOME QUESTIONS OF LAW AND MORALITY

"You can't legislate morality!" There is of course some truth in this aphorism. But if the great majority of decent citizens agree that something is immoral and antisocial, it is not only possible but usually necessary for legislature, courts and executives to strengthen the majority's hands against the miscreants: perpetrators of murder, robbery, perjury, arson, libel. . . .

In an address given at the National Interreligious Convocation on Civil Rights in Washington, D.C., April 1964, Rabbi Uri Miller, then President of the Synagogue Council of America, indicated the false premise on which legislation for morality is frequently opposed. It is often maintained that one must wait until people are educated to the desired attitude; but he said that education and law, far from being mutually exclusive, depend to a large degree upon each other. We must demonstrate, he said, that "law is the one way civilized communities have found to make effective the moral will of the community." His address drew effectively and eloquently upon Judaism's well-known reliance upon the Law and its faithful observance.

Attempts to legislate Prohibition in the 1920's failed on the national scale because there was substantial difference of opinion among generally law-abiding citizens as to the permissibility of drinking. There are still some areas in the country where the sale of alcoholic drinks is prohibited. The cause of temperance, however, finds some legislative and administrative support in licensing laws, the regulation of closing hours, and prevention of sales to minors. There are also laws against drinking while driving; here, of course, public safety as well as morality is involved. While temperance seems likely to be promoted more directly by education than by legislation, it may become necessary in an industrial age to guarantee sobriety at many controls besides those of automobiles.

SUNDAY CLOSING LAWS

A good many states have Sunday closing laws for ordinary commerce. These work hardships on Sabbatarians engaged in commerce, and to some extent on those who refuse to buy on their Sabbath but would gladly purchase on Sunday. There seems to be a growing tendency to recognize these hardships, and in some cases to permit shops that are closed on Saturday to open on Sunday. Much of the support for the Sunday closing drive is humane rather than strictly religious (although also supported by religion) based, namely, on the need for a day of rest. Greater flexibility in this matter has been made possible by the practically universal adoption of the five-day week in the United States.

A 1962 Background Report written for the Project by Philip Perlmutter of the Boston office of the American Jewish Committee is devoted to "Massachusetts Sunday Laws and the Sabbatarian Issue." Liberalization of the Sunday closing laws in Massachusetts was defeated when the Senate, influenced, Mr. Perlmutter thinks, by an editorial in the Catholic Boston *Pilot,* rescinded its earlier action. He reports from a community relations analysis of the Massachusetts situation that certain conceptual guidelines are emerging as to how needless intergroup, interreligious misunderstanding might be prevented. He finds that, while group pressures are to be expected in a pluralistic society, they may be in some measure reduced by the methods of dialogue if undertaken well in advance of a legislative decision, before lines have hardened. When the ultimate decision rests with the courts, it is the responsibility of community groups to create a climate of sobriety and respect. Derogatory implications are not to be deduced from the attitude of a group on a particular matter, e.g., opposition to exemptions for Jewish Sabbatarians does not have to be anti-Semitic. Nor are those who favor exemptions for Saturday Sabbatarians necessarily foes of Sunday observance. "Religious groups of the majority, or minority, should not become political instruments whereby other groups are impeded or injured in the pursuit of religious freedom." Legislators should be chosen to represent not a religious faction, but the community as a whole.

GAMBLING: FOR PLEASURE AND FOR GOVERNMENT REVENUE

The population seems to be deeply divided on the question of the prevention or even regulation of *gambling*. Those who uphold gambling seem to regard it as a purely private matter, and even for the individual merely a question of how much he can afford to lose. Since this viewpoint opens the way for the professional gambler, it would seem to make him a socially approved figure, while many others would consider him completely antisocial. There is no known way of restricting gambling to those who can afford it, or to the amount they can afford to lose. The professional or otherwise successful gambler encourages others to gamble—more those who desperately need to gain than others. Gambling is antisocial in that it encourages the idea and the desire of securing income with no corresponding service to society. The professional gambler's experience and skill distort the calculable odds—as when a professional athlete enters a contest with amateurs.

SEXUAL MORALITY AND LAW

There are a considerable number of issues involving in one way or another, and in different degrees, relations between the sexes. The question of multiple wives (simultaneously!) would seem to have been settled by the conditions upon which Utah was admitted to the Union. It may well be argued that polygamy was introduced in order to hasten the increase in the number of adherents to a new religion, and also to add rapidly to the number of workers in an agrarian community. On that basis one might say that there was no real question of religious liberty involved in stipulating that polygamy could not be practiced within the United States. However, whatever the grounds in policy for introducing the practice, it became a matter of faith and loyalty for many of the Latter Day Saints, some of whom emigrated beyond our borders in order to live according to their faith. This may well be a case where the "public order" is in genuine conflict with religious liberty. (One could mention the family of Governor George Romney; he was born in Mexico.)

The matter of divorce would seem to be as nearly one where you can't legislate morality as we are likely to find. However, either laws that are too strict or laws that are not strict enough may themselves be substantially immoral, in the one case encouraging hypocrisy and perjury, in the other irresponsible marriage. A law that permits a divorce when the parties find it impossible to live together cannot very well prevent remarriage without involving the authorities in a kind of moral inquisition. Only the kind of education (which may be buttressed by religion) that leads young people to enter into marriage with the expectation and resolution that it is for life seems likely to reduce the number of divorces and broken homes.

Sexual deviation seems to be increasingly regarded as a matter more for medicine and psychotherapy than for legislature or courts. As more is known, however, education must play its part in bringing about the kind and degree of understanding and toleration that are compatible with the welfare both of the deviates and of the public.

Planned parenthood and a phenomenal increase in the world's population must be considered not only in the setting of this chapter, but in a later chapter in relation to world peace. In the 1962 meeting under the auspices of the Project in New York City, a paper on planned parenthood was presented. The Reverend Dean Kelley presented the problem of "birth control" as a point of departure for the discussion of law and morality. Rejecting the acrimonious debate with imputation of unworthy motive as a method that leads away from the truth, he specified some of the conditions for fruitful dialogue in the given area. If the opposing protagonists, usually Protestants and Roman Catholics, accept each other's sincerity, eliminating such implications as lustfulness on the one hand and "biological imperialism" on the other, assume a genuine moral concern as actuating the opposition, and grant that the only real question dividing the two groups is that of the best method of being truly "responsible parents," then the moral-religious division may be reduced to the minimum. Mr. Kelley cited twenty-three conclusions concerning artificial birth control from the Catholic writer Norman St. John-Stevas. We note a few of them:

The use of contraceptives is a normally accepted practice by the majority in England and America. Their sale in England is generally unrestricted, but is restricted by federal law in the United States. Many states prohibit their sale and advertisement; some, advertisement only. Such restrictions are not contrary to the Federal Constitution. The restrictions are effective principally in Connecticut and Massachusetts; in the former a statute attempts to forbid their use. Christian opinion is united in approving family planning but divided over the moral legitimacy of certain methods. Roman Catholics and Eastern Orthodox consider contraception contrary to the law of God. Catholics consider it contrary to the natural law which is binding on all men; they sanction the rhythm method.

St. John-Stevas thinks Catholics would be unwise to attempt to secure a total legislative ban on contraceptives, and condemns the Connecticut statute in particular. He sees no way of reconciling the conflict of principle as to whether tax-supported hospitals should be allowed to dispense birth-control advice; only a compromise is possible, such as that used in New York City hospitals: advice to be given only if medically necessary, and employees exempted from participation on conscientious grounds.

World population growth requires a concerted international effort to raise living standards. The author would see more hope in this if the race did not have to begin so far behind any tolerable starting point. Multiplied millions decade after decade have suffered from a subnormal diet; they still do. St. John-Stevas favors emigration as a partial alleviation of the population problem. He would not make our foreign aid conditional on the adoption of artificial birth-control policies, and is convinced that the United Nations can maintain no policy except neutrality with regard to contraception.

Dean Kelley observed that "religion is not the sole or sufficient source or guarantor of morality, but it cannot be denied that the religious posture, movement, institution has as one of its main traits, effects, or functions, the forming, inculcating, and expressing of normative judgments: should's and ought's and must's."

As to the legislation of morality, whose efficacy is obviously limited, "the laws must grow out of and reflect a certain degree of moral consensus, without which they go unenforced. . . ." Perhaps the law's most educational feature is to be found in the categories in which the law is framed: "if these assume a certain structure in society, such as segregation, it will tend to be assumed by all, whether they obey or not." As to those who maintain that society as a whole must be improved before you can deal with a particular miscreant, Mr. Kelley remarks that their recommendation is "to cure the whole society at once, starting nowhere in particular first."

The same speaker drew attention to an important distinction:

the disputed acts of devotion in public schools are religious per se; birth control, though contrary to some consciences, is not in itself a religious practice.

During the discussion representatives of the Planned Parenthood Federation of America, Inc., acknowledged that their organization had acquired a reputation as being anti-Catholic, but that their position was not necessarily or intentionally so. (About the same time a similar attempt to correct that situation was made by a statement to the Vatican.) Also, Father Robert F. Drinan, S.J., indicated that Catholic opposition to the repeal of the Connecticut statute was unwise; this opinion has been later confirmed by statements from the office of Cardinal Cushing. The U.S. Supreme Court in 1965 found the Statute unconstitutional. It begins to look as though real dialogue is progressing and can progress in this country as to the function of the legislature with regard to planned parenthood.

Internationally the chief controversy at present seems to be among Roman Catholics themselves. While "the pill" was much talked of in and around the Third Session of the Second Vatican Council, and vigorous pleas were uttered by influential prelates for thoughtful reconsideration of the Church's teaching and policy with regard to responsible parenthood, pronouncement must come from the Supreme Pontiff. He appointed a Commission in 1964, outside the Council structure, to consider whether an oral contraceptive might be used without contravening the moral law. The Commission was not able to agree on a report which would justify any change in Catholic teaching in time for Pope Paul to issue a statement by the time the Council adjourned. He has confessed to real perplexity on the subject. Some of the perplexity on the subject seems to be due to scientific uncertainty rather than to the theologians. Early in 1966, Pope Paul reorganized the Commission.

The Archbishop of York, according to *Religious News Service* (April 20, 1965), has stressed the need for birth control to cope with "the terrifying" rise in the world's population. He was speaking before the Yorkshire Institute of Agriculture to indicate the urgency of increased food production.

Many Protestant leaders and Protestant bodies could be cited to the effect that birth control not only is not contrary to the will of God, but is often necessary in order to comply with that will. For example, the National Council of Churches has said:

> Our Lord was concerned about children. He would not be happy to see millions of children diseased, hungry, uneducated, uncared for, and unwanted simply because of the irresponsibility of their parents. Children should not be brought into the world unless they can receive the care to which they are entitled. It is an evil thing to perpetuate and aid methods that spawn, even as animals are spawned, millions of human beings for whom there is no adequate support.
>
> Parents need to remember that having children is a venture in faith, requiring a measure of courage and confidence in God's goodness. Too cautious a reckoning of the costs may be as great an error as failure to lift the God-given power of procreation to the level of ethical decision.

The New York Times of April 21, 1965, reported that Ex-Senator Keating will head a new agency to lobby in Washington for improvement in population control measures. Earlier in the month the United Nations Population Commission approved a plan to expand the United Nations role in all areas of population research, including promotion of birth control and family planning activities. (*Religious News Service,* April 8, 1965)

CENSORSHIP

Much has been written on censorship. Various attempts have been made to devise a form of censorship that will not do more harm than good. The aim is usually to prevent communication that stimulates immorality, particularly sexual immorality, or violence.

The first difficulty is to establish with convincing certainty that the films, broadcasts, magazines, books, or pictures in question actually lead to immorality or crime.

Another difficulty is to decide whether the primary problem is not that of curbing the demand rather than—or more than—that of limiting the supply.

Also, it is dangerous to give either to official or voluntary bodies the function of interfering with freedom to view, to read, to listen. Why not undertake to limit lewd, profane or otherwise objectionable conversation by Big Brother, some Gestapo, or other police? Pope Paul decided that the censorship authority of the Sacred Congregation of the Holy Office had to be reduced.

It is increasingly evident that the advocates and practitioners of censorship bring more loss by curbing freedom than gain by trying to curb distasteful and demoralizing communication.

A notable gain has been achieved by a shift of emphasis from denunciation of the bad to recommendation of the good by the Catholic Legion of Decency. Correspondingly, the name was changed to the National Catholic Office for Motion Pictures. The Methodist *Christian Advocate* welcomed the change to a positive approach, and called for an increase in affirmative Protestant action.

Our real remedy is the education of the individual to choose for himself. He can be aided through objective evaluation by competent critics of what is offered to the public, through book reviews, film classifications, etc. He can be aided by producers who have the courage to accept the economic risk of supplying less that is bad, or valueless, and more that merits attention. Chiefly, he himself must learn to choose.

CAPITAL PUNISHMENT

Many years ago, under the influence of Beccaria, Italy led the way in the abolition of capital punishment. There is much argument pro and con as to the deterrent effect on others by example, and on the potential murderer himself, of laws inflicting the death penalty. In medieval Europe such laws extended even to some petty crimes against property, but now they usually apply only to premeditated homicide and to treason. It would be difficult to prove that the infliction of capital punishment tends to increase respect for human life in the general public rather than to its cheapening, especially when legal executions are widely publicized or even presented as spectacles to a somewhat morbid public. It is perhaps too much to hope that religious bodies will consider it their responsibility to raise the sharp question whether human beings have the right to take the life of one of their number, as long as most religious bodies support or acquiesce in their nation's wars involving wholesale slaughter. If they faced squarely the question of capital punishment, it might strengthen their conscientious opposition to war.

There seems to be a trend among the states of the Union to abolish capital punishment. There have been church statements calling for such abolition, but the movement thus far seems to rest more on general humanitarian grounds, and doubt as to the efficacy of capital punishment, than upon profound religious conviction. England recently decided to abolish it.

The questions listed and briefly discussed in this chapter as church and state or religion and government concerns are that, but they are more. They are concerns of society, of all the people. A narrowly conceived compromise to resolve an immediate issue between agencies of government and religion may prove to be antisocial. Not only so: people as a whole must in many cases be carefully prepared to accept and carry out an agreement that in itself is ideal, but involves changes in their habits and attitudes. This would be evident if religious leaders were agreed on ideal solutions to questions in this chapter: it is startlingly and painfully evident in the problems considered in the next two chapters: racial prejudice and anti-Semitism.

6

RELIGION AND RACE

"The Southern way of life" has been increasingly revealed as a
snare and a delusion not only for the South but for the nation.
What sense it made rested on a practical monopoly of the chief
crops, especially cotton, and cheap labor in a patrician, benevo-
lently paternalistic and essentially agrarian society, with the benefit
of a supposedly inexhaustible rich soil. That soil has washed away
from a large part of the cotton-producing territory. The cheap
labor is being more and more replaced by machinery. The cotton
monopoly has been largely eroded. The benevolence which sometimes lubricated human relations in a plantation economy was
inextricably identified with a paternalism which is completely out
of place in an urban and industrial setting. Paternalism could be
and was tolerated for decades only by those Negroes who saw no
escape from a servile position, and had neither the qualifications
needed for any alternative situation nor the social organization to
seek out, develop, prepare for and take advantage of alternative
employment.

Efforts to improve the situation between Emancipation and the
Second World War failed, on the whole, to come to grips with the
underlying realities. The benevolent efforts of white people, some
by Northern churches, some by Southern churches and some by
voluntary organizations with Christian inspiration and leadership
were geared, perhaps inevitably, to gradualism. After World War
I, stimulated by the supposed menace of returning Negro service-
men, these efforts were oriented toward equality, but they were on

115

too small a scale. If left to themselves, sound as their intent was, these efforts would scarcely have availed to avert disaster. The National Association for the Advancement of Colored People did valiant work against lynching and other abuses, both through research and publicity and through the courts. They were aided by white Southern church women, who succeeded in convincing sheriffs in a great many counties that they would not be re-elected if they permitted a lynching in the territories under their supervision.

The Commission on Interracial Cooperation, founded and led by white and Negro Christians, did distinguished research work and helped to promote communication, in an atmosphere of equality and reciprocal trust, in many schools and churches and to some extent in the field of labor. They were mainly Protestants, but there was distinguished Catholic participation. It has been succeeded by the Southern Regional Council. Important foundation work of the same general nature was done by the Student Christian Associations and the Fellowship of Reconciliation. White and Negro Student Christian Associations succeeded in the '20's and the '30's in unifying their regional Councils and student Conferences, and helped to found local interracial student and faculty Councils in a number of Southern cities. Students enlisted and trained in these Councils are still giving leadership nationally and locally in interracial relations. But the active and united leadership of churches and synagogues in the field of race relations was to come a generation later. Individual Jews, at many places in the South that could be specified, are active in befriending Negroes and aiding in the struggle for civil rights. To name them would be to handicap their efforts and expose them to personal and group peril.

Negro leaders at the "grass roots" were to be found chiefly as pastors of Negro churches and as teachers and, gradually, as administrators in Negro schools. They were always caught in the dilemma of abandoning the institutions of religion and education or of perpetuating segregation. They could not achieve institutional autonomy because they were still dependent in large degree on contributions from white people and the toleration, however grudg-ing, of the white power structure. The battle against illiteracy, poverty and the acceptance of paternalism was waged vigorously, and with constantly growing success, by the NAACP, the Urban League and the Negro press.

Difficulties were compounded by the demagoguery of white poli-ticians. In several of the Southern states it would have been almost fatal to a politician to waver from a patronizing benevolence in the direction of fairness and human dignity. Candidates for office could always obtain a hearing, and were frequently elected when they had no visible qualifications for the office sought except their supposed symbolizing of the Southern way of life, whose most typical slogan was "keep the Negro in his place."

SEPARATE AND EQUAL

Another snare and delusion was the doctrine that the United States Constitution demanded no more than the equality of sepa-rate racial accommodations. The doctrine was established by a verdict of the Supreme Court in the Plessy case in the '90's. The pragmatic fallacy would have been glaringly exposed if any serious effort had been made to apply the doctrine. The Plessy case arose with regard to railway passengers, but was eagerly and perhaps inevitably used to defend segregation in various fields. There was one dissent, by Mr. Justice Harlan, but it was not until 1954 that the Supreme Court revised the doctrine and applied the revision to condemn school segregation.

Actually to duplicate facilities of equal comfort and value in transportation, in education, and in merchandising would have been enormously expensive. Also, for a generation or two much of the service on behalf of Negroes would have had to be performed by white people, with the inevitable confirmation and preservation of the theory of white superiority.

But the most pernicious aspect of the separate and equal doc-trine is the recognition of any basis for a demand for separation in a society supposedly governed by the principles of the Declaration of Independence and the Constitution of the United States, to say nothing of the underlying assumptions in the Judeo-Christian tradition.

INTEGRATION OR EDUCATION?

Education was long considered by the foes of segregation and of the inferior status of Negroes as the eventually necessary and effective, and indeed the only conceivable, remedy. Education of course is necessary, and one need not in any sense discount the sincerity, the courage and the generosity of those leaders, Negro and white, who devoted themselves to Negro education, both to extend it and improve its quality. But education alone would not and will not suffice, and in any case was too slow: *segregated* education as the one road to integration was almost as chimerical as pie in the sky.

On the other hand, integration as a judicial and commercial process and goal is hopeless without education. Integration overnight would mean the entrance of Negroes into the social fabric on the same basis as whites, but most of them in that case would be in the category of "poor whites." Integration does not educate and education does not integrate: each alone could only open a distant and doubtful door for the other. Gradualism is thus doubly damned in the eyes of the Negro and of any true friend. Education and integration must go hand in hand, and if both are not accelerated to a revolutionary speed with the support of all Americans, North and South, wholesale tragedy cannot be long postponed— or, should we not say, soon terminated: we are prone to recognize tragedy only when its perennial victims resort to riots.

The need for speed is underscored by several factors, and is increasingly understood even by those who until recently were indifferently moderate in their racial attitudes. The 1954 Supreme Court decision warned reactionaries that segregation, however warmly defended as an essential ingredient of the Southern way of life, could no longer be defended as the American way. Many who saw their sentiments outraged, their power and prestige undermined, began to react with a desperation in sharp and eloquent contrast to their somewhat amused toleration or indifference toward the voluntary efforts to which we referred above.

Nowadays there are Negro leadership and Negro organizations which have won their spurs and are a rallying point and a symbol in the whole Civil Rights struggle. Negroes have become confident of taking their proper place in American life as did the earlier waves of Irish, German, Italian and Slavic immigrants. They have the advantage, and most of them are ready to claim it, of sharing the American heritage: they have been Americans more than two centuries; they know it and feel it. A Negro high school boy in Texas in the 1920's was heard to say, regarding his Hi-Y organization, "We can change our constitution just as *our forefathers* provided for the amendment of the American Constitution": he both claimed and exercised the American heritage.

There are more and more situations in which Negroes, as fast as they become registered voters, will have significant political weight, in some cases a balance of power.

The achievement of independence by colored populations in two score African states and the rise to independence and power of native non-white populations throughout Asia must give pause to white supremacists, and great encouragement to those who believe that all God's children are going to have not only shoes, harps and wings in the next life, but self-respect, their democratic share of power, and the respect of all men, in this life.

THE SOUTH VICTIMIZED

The South has been victimized by outside agencies and by circumstances over which it had no control, both by the importation of slaves and by the willingness of outside capital to take advantage of the promise of cheap labor. While the cheap labor yielded certain advantages in the short run, especially for agricultural employers, its advantage for industry has been doubtful, and in some cases it has been obviously a disadvantage. Cheap and submissive labor has never been of net advantage to the nation or to the South itself. It has resulted in a severe limitation of the Southern market. Cheap labor is not able to buy. Illiterate labor has few demands. Over thirty years ago the able superintendent of Atlanta schools observed that "third graders do not eat olives." Cheap labor is nonprogressive and relatively impotent. It invites exploitative capital. Workers' unions can invade the field of cheap labor only at great immediate cost and risk. Thus in many localities in the South the unions have not only accepted but defended segregation, thereby weakening themselves and the whole union movement. On the whole it is true that the South itself has exploited cheap labor and has thus become the principal victim of the exploitation.

BUT THE PROBLEM IS NATIONAL

Not only does the North share heavily in the responsibility for the importation of Negro labor and in its exploitation through some three hundred years; the North has permitted the development of a stubborn *de facto* segregation, and white people in the North, many of whom are of fairly recent immigrant origin, do not share the tradition of responsibility which the better Southerners feel, and which in spite of its paternalistic inadequacy was for many decades a cushion that lessened interracial friction. It is thus timely and just that both Dr. Martin Luther King's movement, the Southern Leadership Conference, and the National Council of Churches' Commission on Religion and Race are extending their field of action to Northern cities. There are also various strong local groups working for the improvement of race relations in many Northern cities. Outstanding, perhaps, is the Catholic activity in Chicago.

The South, one is bound to say, and as a Southerner is glad to say, does not present a uniformly hopeless picture, just as the North is not uniformly free of trouble or blame. Pointing to others' shortcomings, be it noted, offers neither justification nor remedy for our own. Though it may serve to diminish an area's public shame, it is sheer demagoguery for a politician to defend one region by pointing to the defects of another, and it is moral turpitude for citizens of either region to accept its faults with complacency because the other is equally or more guilty. The impressive efforts of many white and Negro Southerners during the past five decades to maintain communication with each other, to cooperate in the improvement of education, and to arouse their neighbors and their churches to move in the same direction, have not gone for naught. They now have business, the Supreme Court, Congress, and national church leadership on their side. Southerners may resist legal changes, but the vast majority intend to be law-abiding. The picture is also improving because Negroes have able leadership, intelligent and amazingly restrained and disciplined masses of followers, fresh courage and new hope. Their wisdom in resisting the blandishments of Communist agitators and in avoiding mass violence has been phenomenal. Their churches have given both shelter and strength.

The excellent but inadequate efforts of the two decades following World War I pricked the conscience of many white Southerners. Now, however, a new factor with almost irresistible force begins to be felt: segregation costs commercially far more than it is worth. This is not due to artificially stimulated boycotts, but to the self-victimization to which we referred above. This increasingly felt cost must aid religion to overcome an inadequacy of opportunity and enjoyment for Negroes in the United States that may be broken down into five areas: civil rights, education, housing, employment, and community and personal acceptance.

CIVIL RIGHTS

It is in the field of civil rights, perhaps, that combined religious forces in the United States are now making their principal collective contribution, and that religion is doing most to merit the respect of the man in the street for its contribution to a free society. One may say, and it has been said vigorously, that this effort is too little and too late. It may be so little and so late that it will not go far enough to wipe out the wretched record of a hundred years of relative inertia since the Emancipation Proclamation. However, certain efforts of religious bodies as such on behalf of Negroes and of better race relations must be noted, even before the National Conference on Religion and Race convened in Chicago in 1963. "Missionary" efforts in the South by Congregationalists and others resulted in the founding of secondary schools and colleges. Some Southern denominations did the same sort of missionary work. Thus we had for many decades denominationally supported schools, some drawing their support mainly from the North, others from the South. They were not always segregated. Berea College in Kentucky was in fact segregated only a comparatively short time before its recent desegregation—it was, however, primarily a school for white students—but in recent decades segregation was statutory across the South. Education was also aided by Jewish philanthropists, helping institutions directly, and setting up foundations (e.g., the Rosenwald Fund) for more general aid.

In 1963, thanks in part to a new ecumenical climate to which Pope John and the Second Vatican Council largely contributed, official bodies representing the three major faiths held a conference in Chicago and formed an organization, The National Conference on Religion and Race. While the new organization has largely surrendered its functions to the bodies that created it, the continued cooperation of the three faiths in the racial field, and the spur given to individual denominations, has been much more than episodic: it may well prove yet to be epic. There is abundant testimony from religious leaders themselves as to the beneficial influence of this new-found cooperation.

While the civil rights bill was pending, a tremendous ecumenical and interracial rally was held at Georgetown University, where Senator Humphrey was an applauded visitor. He had, as floor manager for the civil rights bill, said that its passage "depends in large part on the activity of the churches." This was in March. In June, after the filibuster had been halted by cloture, the Senator recognized on the Senate floor that church groups and leaders had played a significant part in arousing the American conscience, treating "this great issue of human rights as not primarily a political or partisan issue, but fundamentally a religious and moral question." The Senator had received unanimous Senate consent to insert in *The Congressional Record* Pope John's entire encyclical on peace, *Pacem in Terris*.

President Johnson had also credited churchmen for their past participation in the civil rights drive and called on them to continue their support: "So help us in this hour. Help us to see and do what must be done. Inspire us with renewed faith. Stir our consciences. Strengthen our will. Inspire and challenge us to put our principles into action. For the future of our faith is at stake, and the future of this nation is at stake." Senator Javits declared that the influence of religious groups might well make the difference between an effective civil rights bill and a washed-out one. Now, some months later, there is already visible encouraging and widespread compliance with the Civil Rights Act, but churches and synagogues are well aware that continuing vigilance is imperative. The National Council of Churches, through its representatives at Congressional hearings, was sufficiently effective that Senator Strom Thurmond, while still a Democrat, charged it with lobbying and resultant jeopardy to its status as a tax-exempt organization. However, the Senator did not point out any activity more definitely of a lobbying nature than the issuance of a letter calling on constituents to be watchful and to support the bill vigorously.

Among those praising religious organizations of all faiths for their leadership in race relations was Governor Connally of Texas who said, "Brotherhood demands initiative, understanding demands concern, love demands work." More recently, Senator Robert Kennedy of New York has said that the civil rights bill of 1965 would not have passed without the active support that it received from the churches. Senator Richard Russell of Georgia has acknowledged—and deplored—the same fact.

Negroes and other minority racial groups are not likely to enjoy other civil rights and citizenship privileges in anything like full measure until they not only have the right to vote, but exercise it. Retroactive poll taxes, restricted opportunities for applying for registration, unfair administration of literacy tests have been among the devices used to disfranchise Negroes across the South as effectively as "the grandfather clause" did for many years. This was a clause which satisfied the officials of one's right to vote if one's grandfather did! Even after it was effectively disposed of for the stated and final elections, attempts were made to use it and to justify it legally in the primary elections of the Democratic Party which were actually decisive, but which were represented before the federal courts as private affairs similar to club elections. The federal courts began to strike down this pretense in the late '20's.

One great difficulty has been to persuade Negroes that it was worth the necessary effort to register and vote. In the '30's one friend of the author in North Carolina, by his personal efforts over two or three years, induced no fewer than one thousand Negroes to effect their registration; North Carolina, however, did not impose the effective barriers to registration that are still met in Alabama and Mississippi and some other states. Congress in 1965 produced a fair and enforceable Act which in a few years could right many of the wrongs now prevalent in the field of franchise: prospects for its enforcement are encouraging.

Here again churchmen individually and collectively have been and are vigorous. James Reston in his *New York Times* column (March 19, 1965) credits particularly "the new generation of clergymen and students" for helping to turn the tide in Selma, Alabama. He credits also the National Council of Churches and the National Catholic Council for Racial Justice for effective support in the civil rights conflict, as if it were what William James called "the moral equivalent of war." Reston continued, "This rights protest in the nation is having its effect and promises to help transform the voting laws."

EDUCATION

One of the civil rights whose enjoyment is necessary in order to give full values to the others is the right to enjoy the same facilities in education that are enjoyed by others. Theoretically this might be realized through "equal and separate" facilities. In practice this has not been realized and is almost impossible of realization. Nevertheless, it is arguable that any aid to education for Negroes which can be made available without increasing discrimination should be accepted, since the long-term acquisition of equal status will be greatly dependent on the education of the minority. This is, one hopes, an interim question only. The interim, however, is long and painful. Since the Supreme Court decision in 1954 striking down racial segregation in public schools, progress has been slow throughout the nation, and there are a few places where no progress has yet been registered. The Supreme Court decision seemed applicable primarily, if not exclusively, to the situation in Southern states. Actually, however, there is *de facto* segregation in Northern cities, due mainly to segregated housing.

As in the case of public transportation, separate facilities would never really be equal: the duplication of equipment, especially where taxes are voted by a resisting white majority, would always be an obstacle. Compliance with the 1954 ruling has been encouraging in several border states, and may be expected eventually throughout the nation. Meanwhile, millions of children have only substandard schooling.

On a separate-but-equal basis, some of the Southern states have taxed themselves at a high rate for education including the education of Negroes, but the tax base is woefully inadequate, especially in poorer agricultural areas, where a one-crop system has impoverished the soil and sharecropping has kept many thousands of Negro families at bare subsistence level. Children ill-clothed, undernourished, and taken out of school in the busy spring and autumn seasons, and too often with a home background that inspires them with no hope or ambition, remain in the same grade two or three terms, until they become discouraged or pass beyond the age when attendance is required.

As a Southerner, the author has never been able to understand why every advocate of better race relations has not been also an advocate of federal aid to education, provided especially that it not be used in a way to prolong segregation. One is inclined to sing the Doxology or the *Te Deum* now that the traditional barrier to federal aid has been at least in part surmounted. The new ecumenical climate, cooperation between Catholics and Protestants in many communities and at national level, and vigorous leadership by the Federal Government all deserve grateful recognition. The proof of the pudding is still to be found in the eating. There is evidence, however, that a great majority of the national leadership, religious and secular, is determined to see that the Act is properly implemented. This will require reasonable regulations in administration by the Department of Health, Education and Welfare, and there is encouraging evidence that we may count on these.

Careful preparation, community by community and state by state, is also necessary, and here both the churches and the schools have inescapable responsibilities and challenging opportunities. The prejudices, the discrimination, the tyranny indulged in by the white majority—or by the power structures with the majority's acquiescence or complacent indifference amounting to approval— will not disappear merely because of legislation. It will not yield rapidly enough by court action. Law and its enforcement are indispensable. But habits and attitudes sanctified for generations by practice and rationalization—and even by misquoted or misunderstood Bible texts—will not be abandoned unless both the mind and the heart are changed. The school, the press, the pulpit, the Sunday-school—all must join to bring about fundamental changes that in millions of cases must transform the personality as profoundly as a religious conversion.

One should not dismiss this area of our subject without pointing out that it is not only Negroes who suffer from segregation. In the South especially, segregation has permitted white children to grow

up with the unchallenged assumption that their race had made
them superior, so that a white boy felt no need to study. He was
already superior! He did not need to vote; his vote was counted in
advance for the one who guaranteed his superiority; he did not
need to join a union, for the Klan could turn colored people out of
jobs to make room for him. He did not need athletics or recreation; he could demonstrate his prowess and have his fun by bully-
ing an "inferior." The whole system of segregation has now for
more than a hundred years demonstrated the truth of Booker
Washington's famous observation that "in order to hold a man in
the ditch it is necessary to stay in the ditch with him." You can
even do so complacently!

HOUSING

Much of the segregation in the schools and some of that in the
churches has a close correlation with segregation in housing. Segregation in housing usually and almost naturally means discrimination in public utilities. The transportation services to the ghettos
are likely to be of inferior quality, sewers and water mains to be
inadequate, and the lighting and the paving and the cleaning of the
streets to be substandard or nonexistent. This may be true even
where Negroes have the franchise; it is certain to be true where
they do not.

The ghetto rests on the twin supports of prejudice and poverty;
it tends to increase both, and the increase dooms the ghetto to
perpetuation. Then those who can, flee to the suburbs. There poverty and prejudice together and separately combine to keep Negroes out, and we have the ghetto in reverse, with the difference
that its citizens are not only complacently satisfied but dedicatedly
determined to perpetuate it! Even those economically privileged
white residents who do not flee to the suburbs tend to send their
children to private schools, not necessarily under religious auspices, and this again perpetuates the ghetto attitude. It is idle to
criticize those who flee from the ghetto in either manner. The

problem is to eliminate the ghettos. Where the flight to the suburbs is not in full swing, something may be done to prevent its occurring, and here the churches and synagogues have a responsibility and an opportunity.

A new ghetto is frequently formed when a few Negroes move into a previously white community, and panic ensues among the property owners. This panic may be spontaneous, though based on false assumptions, or it may be inspired and accelerated by speculators. In a few cases across the nation there have been successful efforts, with churches and synagogues cooperating, to convince white property owners that Negro neighbors would not represent a decrease in property values or other deteriorations in community life, and Negroes have bought property and moved in with results which justified the efforts and the insights of those who on a voluntary cooperative basis had organized the fair-housing campaign. It is almost impossible to calm the apprehensions of white residents except by cooperative action, enlisting a substantial number of the owners in the given area. It has been often demonstrated that pronouncements and resolutions by religious bodies are ineffective in this field without the persistent community follow-up. In 1964 nineteen states had laws against discrimination in some types of public housing; none of those were in the South, and not all of them were effective. *The New York Times* (March 27, 1965), in an article based on information from the National Committee Against Discrimination in Housing, reported that seven additional states were considering fair-housing bills for the first time. The Committee reported more favorable reaction from legislatures than from referendums, and suggested that realty interests sometimes promote the referendum as a means of avoiding legislation. The Indiana legislature had recently defeated a proposal for a referendum and passed a bill with broad coverage against housing discrimination which was signed into law on March 9.

On the other hand, fair-housing laws have been recently defeated or repealed when subjected to referendum. In 1964 in California church bodies and church leaders separately and unitedly proclaimed their support of the 1963 Rumford Act which prohibited discrimination in the sale, rental or financing of many types of housing. But in a state-wide referendum supported by realty interests and others, the law was repealed by a margin of almost two to one, with the proviso that the legislature could in future enact no new fair-housing law without referendum approval. In May 1966, the California Supreme Court, on the basis of the Fourteenth Amendment (federal), nullified the referendum vote. The city of Detroit in 1964 passed a "home owners' rights ordinance" which in effect recognizes racial discrimination in housing. The vote was about 6 to 5, although the governor, the mayor and many religious, labor and other community organizations had opposed the ordinance. In New Mexico a fair-housing bill was defeated in the House of Representatives, despite its support by almost all religious groups in the state.

The record is not encouraging as to church influence. This is partly due to the fact that the churches have only recently entered this fray. They have apparently overestimated the readiness of the laity to follow the clergy, and have at any rate not yet done the necessary work of education and persuasion to add voting force to their resolutions. But the churches and synagogues have now resolutely and nationally entered into the fight for interracial justice. They know well that segregated housing is one of the great injustices, and they will not abandon the battle, nor in the long run will they be defeated.

At national level, Catholic, Jewish and Protestant representatives have for three years urged fair housing legislation on Congress. To their voices, in May 1966, was added that of William J. Levitt before the House Judiciary Committee. His firm had built a town on an originally segregated basis. But he said: "When integration takes place, nothing bad happens. . . . No one really seems to care, after the fact." But builders, he feels, need the uniformity and legal protection afforded by a national statute.

EMPLOYMENT

The enjoyment of civil rights, the franchise, equal opportunities in education, open occupancy for residence: these are all fundamental for all citizens, including of course members of all minority groups. But if, with abolition of all barriers in those areas, a man can still not find employment, what shall it profit him? The new crisis in race relations coincides with a tremendous increase in the number of jobs requiring skills which cannot be acquired by illiterates. Restricted opportunity for education therefore partakes of the crisis atmosphere. Skilled workers in unions, furthermore, become increasingly concerned for restricting the number of apprentices. With the average education of the minority groups below the national average because of restricted and inferior educational opportunities, that they are additionally handicapped for skilled employment is obvious. But there have been many unions, at least locals, throughout the years which erected barriers against Negroes long before the word "automation" became current.

In some sections of the country this was job protection with racial prejudice as a convenient instrument. One union indeed, for Pullman porters, enjoyed a practical monopoly for Negroes! But the leadership of that union has waged a constant battle against racial prejudice and restrictions in the labor movement as a whole. Certainly difficulties have been by no means exclusively those created by the unions or by the workers when not organized. Management has shared in or succumbed to personal and community attitudes, frequently failing to open employment to Negroes even when there was no pressure from the unions, and sometimes when there was, and when there would have been no resistance by the community. To open menial jobs to Negroes and restrict them to such employment is in a sense to add insult to injury. Many Southerners began to discover during World War II that the days of cheap, docile domestic labor, maids and cooks for example, were gone. If they have returned in some measure, it can only be temporary. As minimum wage laws are gradually extended to unskilled employment, and as Negroes increasingly qualify for skilled and semi-skilled tasks, menial labor will either be upgraded or will disappear. A socially necessary task should be a socially respected one. Edward Bellamy in *Looking Backward* was right!

ACCEPTANCE OF MINORITY GROUPS

First of all, let us note that in different parts of the country Puerto Ricans, Mexicans and American Indians undergo much of the same hardship and discrimination that we have noted in the case of Negroes. It is doubtful that the national conscience ever will be, or could be, cleansed of its guilt with respect to the Indians who lived here before the white man came. We still confine many of them to reservations. One tribe, the Senecas, has been having extreme difficulty in obtaining anything like just compensation when forced to abandon their homes to permit the creation of a new lake, industrially important. The right of eminent domain is the necessary, utilitarian right of a majority, that is to say of society as a whole. It must be exercised not only with just compensation to those who are its victims, but with maximum consideration, especially in the case of a group already the victims of centuries of discrimination.

One is glad to note that in April 1965 President Johnson signed a bill providing fifteen million dollars annually for job training for Indians, responding, he said, to one of the major concerns of their leaders. Some 13,000 of the nation's 400,000 American Indians have been assisted by a vocational training program in the years since 1958.

But when minority groups enjoy their civil rights, equal educational opportunity, unrestricted residence, and the same job security as other citizens they may still be, and feel themselves, outcasts, victims of the same prejudice as before, possibly increased by resentment and envy. Jews, of whom we shall speak in the next chapter, could offer poignant and damning evidence on this score. Surely in this area the schools and the churches have a tremendous responsibility and a marvelous opportunity. There are indeed those who think that a kind of bi-racialism might represent a tolerable solution in the field of race relations. Such a solution would be no solution in the field of government, unless we separated into different political areas, each politically independent of the other. On the political side, bi-racialism is pure fantasy. But otherwise it is also completely unrealistic. Desegregation has already gone too far in education, in employment and in business in general for it to be possible to reverse the trend, to turn the clock back, even if it were desirable. Perhaps more important, there is a community of culture, of personal acquaintanceship, of democracy, of social ideals, and of the Judeo-Christian heritage which constitutes the solid beginning of "one nation under God."

The racial problem is indeed a national one. There were no "outsiders" in Selma. The shame of Selma, like the shame of Harlem, is national. The responsibility for Selma, like that for Harlem, is national. The only outsider is the one who attempts to maintain and perpetuate attitudes and conditions which are anti-American because they are antisocial and immoral.

RACIAL SUPERIORITY AND DIVINE RIGHT

There are two anti-American, anti-human demons which will not be cast out without prayer and fasting and patient persistence in the face of a human nature that *can* be changed, by education and divine grace, as by a miracle: too many of us are persuaded of our own racial superiority; too many of us accept the privileges that have long been enjoyed by our race as something in the nature of divine right which we not only will not, but should not, surrender.

In a discussion of race with white students thirty years ago in Tennessee, the discussion leader was helping the group to discover factors in its racial attitudes. He raised the question whether supposed white superiority was a factor. An Alabama boy said, "But *aren't* we superior?" Having discovered earlier that this boy was a genuine admirer of George Washington Carver, the agricultural chemist whose research had so greatly enriched the South, the leader asked him if he felt superior to Dr. Carver. After a second's hesitation, the boy said, "No, I don't." This key to interracial understanding, acquaintance with and respect for individuals of the other race, is missing for most white Southerners (likewise in the North?), but too often is not desired, is shunned and rejected by many who with little effort and a minimum of good will could find it. Reading about Negro leaders may cause one to question his own assumed superiority. It vanishes completely when one has known, for example, such leaders as the Johnsons—Charles, James Weldon and Mordecai—and a score of leaders in the Christian Associations, the churches and the civil rights movement whom one could name, and a host of Negro teachers, pastors and businessmen, with whom any white person could establish acquaintance and friendship if he would.

One who is determined to cling to the privileges of the white race is likely to guard jealously his own assumption of racial superiority from any erosion by reason or experience. All that remains for him is either a spiritual change so profound as to cause him to about-face—or to be left in the rubble heap by the inevitable progress of civilization.

RELIGION'S ROLE IN RACE

If religion is to play any significant part in bringing about world peace for our time and for all time, it is evident that it must make a much greater contribution to race relations, both through the behavior of religiously motivated individuals and through the action of religious bodies, especially in concert. There are now enough pronouncements by denominations and councils, Protestant and Catholic, to serve as ample charters for those who engage officially in promoting racial education, understanding and cooperation, but the attitudes and habits of centuries do not yield readily to pronouncements. Too often also the conscience that constrains religious bodies to make pronouncements is satisfied with the pronouncement!

Religion has often been ignorantly or willfully perverted or fanatically prostituted, with truly demonic effect on race relations. In the '30's, for example, one commonly heard in the South that God had cursed Ham and all his descendants, who presumably were all Negroes. Indefatigable work under the auspices of the Commission on Interracial Cooperation seemed to have effectively exposed the nonsense in both these assertions (it was Noah who cursed Ham), but in the last few years one finds that the same falsehoods have been widely propagandized. They have again been meticulously and effectively disproved—for those who will listen.

The churches must enlist specifically to contribute to the normality and stability of Negro family life. Segregation and other forms of discrimination have weighed heavily on the establishment and maintenance of its integrity. In the spring of 1965 the New York City police distributed widely the message "When Family Life Stops—Delinquency Starts." Negro churches, handicapped as they have been, have nevertheless rendered distinguished service to establish and maintain a normal family life for Negroes. We too often forget that Negro families were ruthlessly damaged by slavery. On the one hand, there was widespread illegitimacy under coercion; on the other, families were broken up when one or more members were sold to other owners. Also, there was no secure occupancy—let alone ownership—of a home.

Both at home and abroad the white churches have too often either condescendingly or unwittingly conducted themselves in such a way as to justify the label of Christianity as "the white man's religion." This was partly due to the dependence of missionaries on colonial governments for permission and protection; partly to the failure of many missionaries to identify with their parishioners of another color and culture; partly to the fact that the missionaries, willy-nilly, were excellent heralds of European and American material progress. In spite of these handicaps, missions both Catholic and Protestant must be credited—and are credited by many leaders, partial and impartial, in both Asia and Africa—with founding schools and hospitals, instilling respect for the individual, and improving the status of women. In all these ways they helped to spur the movements for independence and to prepare people for it. There are likewise many records of an extraordinary identification of the missionary with the people he served. The Christian Associations have done excellent work in enlisting and recognizing native leadership. Latins seem to be in general somewhat less prone to claim a racial superiority than Anglo-Saxons and Nordics. This has perhaps in certain areas meant that Roman Catholics, who predominate among the Latins, have been a bit more ready than Anglo-Saxon and German missionaries to recognize native leaders and to fraternize with them. Islam perhaps, as a missionary religion, has an advantage over Christianity when it comes to identification in Africa and Asia. Until recently it has, however, been definitely backward, owing both to its failure to recognize the equal status of women and to its element of fatalism, in inspiring a sense of dignity and of personal initiative.

At some points Roman Catholicism has been more alert to avoid or correct the errors that we have just mentioned than Protestantism. Catholics can accomplish, at least in the early stages, more by authority than Protestants can. They have made great strides in building colored priests into the hierarchy and advancing them to become bishops and cardinals. In Washington, D.C., where racial pressures are both virulent and conspicuous, Archbishop O'Boyle instituted desegregation of the parochial schools before the 1954 decision of the Supreme Court. There have been other conspicuous examples of such leadership in border and Southern cities and states.

What the churches have to do, of course, is to enlist not just for Negro rights or civil rights, but for human rights. This more and more of them are doing through denominational judicatories, interdenominational councils, and ecumenical combinations. A recent example is the action of Southern Baptists' support for their Christian Life Commission's report, which said:

We hereby affirm our purpose to do what we can with
God's help beginning now to undergird our Christian witness
in missions and evangelism at home and abroad with an
uncompromised and an uncompromising testimony at the
point of race.

The churches must desegregate themselves! They must support
nonviolence, dialogue, negotiation. To do these things they must
often convert their own members to a truly Christian view not only
of love but of justice, so that no member would think of joining the
Ku Klux Klan. Thus converted, any church member investing capital in segregated areas would know that he cannot make a profit by
exploiting his brothers, even in situations where the majority, or
the power structure, would approve it. The churches must themselves have, and must communicate to their members, a sense of
the desperate urgency of establishing democratic and Christian
race relations.

As was indicated earlier, personal acquaintance across racial
lines of separation is indispensable. It is the beginning of better
racial attitudes; it is also necessary for the completion of the reforms called for in this chapter. We must begin by accepting Negroes as human beings, children of God. We continue by accepting
them as fellow citizens, fellow students, and fellow workers. Then
we must accept them as neighbors. But unless we move on not
only to accept but to seek them as friends, we are not only "un-
profitable servants" from a religious viewpoint; we remain in essence antisocial. This has nothing to do with intermarriage across
racial lines any more than the same process has to do with marriage in the same racial group. It really has nothing to do with
anything except our common humanity. For, one blushes to relate,
there are still Americans who cannot quite make up their minds
that a Negro is a human being, and who accept or invent various
fantastic and completely unscientific myths to explain their fears,
bolster their prejudices and assuage their consciences.

No one has expressed more vigorously or more eloquently than the Reverend Martin Luther King, Jr., the justification of Negroes' nonviolent protests against racial injustice and persecution. We quote a few excerpts from his "Letter from Birmingham Jail" (*The Christian Century,* June 12, 1963):

Nonviolent direct action seeks to foster such a tension that a community which has constantly refused to negotiate is forced to confront the issue. It seeks so to dramatize the issue that it can no longer be ignored.

Perhaps it is easy for those who have never felt the stinging darts of segregation to say "Wait." But when you have seen vicious mobs lynch your mothers and fathers at will and drown your sisters and brothers at whim; when you have seen hate-filled policemen curse, kick and even kill your black brothers and sisters with impunity; when you see the vast majority of your twenty million Negro brothers smothering in an air-tight cage of poverty in the midst of an affluent society; when you suddenly find your tongue twisted as you seek to explain to your six-year-old daughter why she can't go to the public amusement park that has just been advertised on television, and see tears welling up when she is told that Funtown is closed to colored children, and see ominous clouds of inferiority beginning to form in her little mental sky, and see her beginning to distort her personality by unconsciously developing a bitterness toward white people; when you have to concoct an answer for a five-year-old son asking, "Daddy, why do white people treat colored people so mean?"; when you take a cross-country drive and find it necessary to sleep night after night in the uncomfortable corners of your automobile because no motel will accept you; when you are humiliated day in and day out by nagging signs reading "white" and "colored"; when your first name becomes "nigger," your middle name becomes "boy" (however old you are) and your last name becomes "John," and your wife and mother are never given the respected title "Mrs.";

when you are harried by day and haunted by night by the fact that you are a Negro, never quite knowing what to expect next, and are plagued with inner fears and outer resentments; when you are forever fighting a degenerating sense of "nobodiness"—then you will understand why we find it difficult to wait.

So often the contemporary church is a weak, ineffectual voice with an uncertain sound. So often it is an archdefender of the status quo. . . .

But the judgment of God is upon the church as never before. If today's church does not recapture the sacrificial spirit of the early church, it will lose its authenticity, forfeit the loyalty of millions, and be dismissed as an irrelevant social club with no meaning for the 20th century.

The occasional notes of optimism in this chapter are relative: they are due to slight improvements over the past and to the winning of opportunities for improvement, not to the completion of the task in any sector. To one who has spent most of his seventy-seven years in the South the progress indeed seems phenomenal— but it has obviously been phenomenally slow. Any degree of complacency smacks of the gradualism which waits while tens of millions of whites continue without compunction to enjoy the fruits of a spurious "superiority," and millions of Negroes die without even glimpsing the promised land from afar.

7

ANTI-SEMITISM

Anti-Semitism is a persistent and damning blot on civilization, at least in the Western—especially in the historically Christian—cultures, but the Jews survive, and their survival has seldom been the result of violence on their part. You may well ask whether their oppressors from Pharaoh to Hitler have ever gained materially or spiritually (!) by the injustice and cruelty visited upon the Jews. The same question, with more reason, must be faced by Christians, and by Christianity as such.

What bond or bonds hold the Jews together, constituting them a people throughout more than three thousand years? It can scarcely be exclusively an ethnic bond. They are not too different from other Semitic peoples. A great number of Russians at one time converted en masse to Judaism. Even in Italy the author was informed by an Italian friend that he could not distinguish Jews from Italians except by their family names—no infallible test.

Thirty-five years ago in a seminar in Florida, one heard a rabbi from Chicago argue brilliantly that the decisive bond uniting the Jews was their culture. While there are distinctive elements in the Jewish culture, it would seem difficult to identify any which are not primarily or secondarily religious. In 1935 when Hitler was consolidating his revolution and the handwriting for Jews was already on the wall, as plain as that at the feast of Belshazzar, the author had the privilege of an hour with Berlin's distinguished and heroic Rabbi Baeck. At that point it was already evident that the rallying focus for the fearful Jewish population in Germany was religion and the synagogue.

139

One might of course somewhat paradoxically argue that Jews are principally identified by their very separateness. But one might also argue endlessly as to how far separateness, clannishness if you will, is cause, and how far it is effect.

If one had a case history with statistics of anti-Semitic phenomena in the United States, the land of the free, in the twentieth century, one would be amazed at the discrimination in hotels, clubs, universities, professional schools and residential areas. Anti-Semitism has been at or near the surface in much of the racist feeling in this country. The Ku Klux Klan, one remembers, is in principle as anti-Semitic as it is anti-Negro. The Frank case in Atlanta early in the century brought out just as despicable evidences of human depravity as the Dreyfus case in France. Fortunately, it was on a smaller stage. The author boarded for a time in the home in Atlanta of one of the lawyers who had defended Frank. The lawyer had left his family there temporarily while he sought to begin a new career far from Atlanta. There is thus abundant reason why Jews even in a country as free as ours, when they remember pogroms in Russia and gas chambers in Germany, can never say or feel with entire confidence, "It couldn't happen here." This is in spite of high-level Jewish participation in the commercial, cultural and civic affairs of our nation and most of its communities. There was similar participation in Germany.

Furthermore, the menace has not disappeared elsewhere in the world. There are frequent eruptions of anti-Semitism in the United States and perhaps more in England, led by dedicated followers of Adolf Hitler, in addition to the potential and half-buried anti-Semitic attitudes of considerable sections of the population. In Argentina there is a politically significant anti-Semitic movement, the "Tacaura"; it can boast of its Roman Catholic chaplain. There is frightening evidence that measures persistently followed in the Soviet Union would lead to what Harold Fey has denominated "Cultural Genocide in Russia" (*The Christian Century*, July 21, 1965). For example, "government pressure and discrimination has reduced the number of synagogues from three thousand to fewer than one hundred." Identity papers carry the word "Jew." It is clear to Dr. Fey that Jews as a "nationality" are denied many of the privileges which belong to that status and are accorded to members of a hundred similar sub-groups. The denial violates the Soviet constitution and the stated policy of the Communist party.

President Johnson, in a message to a rally of fifteen thousand persons in behalf of Jews in Russia, called on the Soviet Union to ease its religious and cultural restrictions against its Jewish people: "We believe that, in the interests of all humanity, the spiritual and cultural heritage of these people should be nurtured and preserved." (*Religious News Service,* June 4, 1965)

Fathers Davis and Culhane, editors of Jesuit *America,* were members of an interfaith group that visited Russia in January 1966. Their report (*America,* February 19, 1966) vividly confirms the earlier picture in Dr. Fey's article, emphasizing the apprehensiveness of Jews in Russia and the lack of freedom of their rabbis.

The well-known hostility of Arab governments to Israel is frequently extended to Zionists and their organizations and leaders outside of Israel. Their opposition is essentially political; there is no inherent hostility between Islam and Judaism.

In line with the subject and purpose of this book, we must look more closely and in some detail at the responsibility of religion, and specifically of Christian bodies and leaders, for creating, maintaining, and now at long last beginning to modify for the better, the climate in which Jews move and have their being. Let it be said at once that however much amendment Christians may now bring about, they can never consider it as adequate atonement for the past.

If we look first as individuals at our own part in perpetuating anti-Semitism, most of us have to confess at least two faults. We have been indifferent or passive, and have not resisted the anti-Semitism that is in our social customs and individual habits. We have used the very word "Jew," and repeated jokes about Jews, probably with no malicious thoughts present in our minds at the moment, but containing and spreading, nevertheless, instruments of anti-Semitism that are malicious in their origin and implications; and all too often, yielding to a momentary annoyance perhaps, we have transferred to a whole people the transgression, or just the peculiarity, of an individual or of a small group.

There was anti-Semitism in the Near East and in the Roman Empire before the Christian era. Christians had some excuse in the days before Constantine for trying to distinguish themselves from those who clung to Judaism, so as to avoid the already existing discrimination or persecution. This was very human but not very Christian! It must have puzzled Roman pagans, who, if they understood the two branches of the followers of the theistic prophets, must have known that Christianity, as a missionary faith, was even more certain than Judaism to revolutionize Roman culture and undermine the "religious" sanctions of the Empire and support of the Emperor himself.

In the meantime anti-Jewish interpretations of the Christian teaching and history were being vigorously pushed by some of the early Christian leaders. Marcion tried unsuccessfully to cut Christianity off from its Old Testament antecedents and to eliminate from the Christian Scriptures anything that tended to establish continuity. Fortunately he was unsuccessful with regard to the canon of the Bible, but he left an inheritance. In the worst days of Mussolini's acquiescence in Hitlerism, we were able at the Y.M.C.A. in Rome to ridicule the performance by presenting a lecture on Marcion. By taking hostile note of this, the Fascists would merely have rendered themselves ridiculous. Another lecture on racism in the United States held up a mirror in which Fascists could not escape the likeness to their own anti-Jewish measures.

Saint John Chrysostom, otherwise one of the truly great Church Fathers, proceeding probably more by way of parable and exegesis than from personal experience, depicted the Jews as Christ's worst enemies, and of course as his executioners. While we have seen at the Second Vatican Council a profound struggle going on to correct, as far as decrees and formulas can do it, the image of Roman Catholicism with regard to the Jews, we may reflect that not all the opposition from Roman Catholic bishops of the Near East patriarchates is political. Much of it is, directly or derivatively, political. Rulers of the Arab states fear and resent the state of Israel, and the Near East prelates may share their fear; they must also have feared reprisals of one sort or another if they did not speak out vigorously against the Council's proposed statement on relations with the Jews. In addition, however, their religious tradition is steeped in the heritage of Saint John Chrysostom and other early Christian teachers.

But it is not only in the Near East that Christianity has preserved and even cultivated the roots and the branches of anti-Semitism. One of the foremost among the Jewish scholars who have examined the Christian teachings in this field was the late Professor Jules Isaac. He in fact made a life work of the examination of Christian teaching and practice with regard to the Jews, publishing works which are classical in the field. In 1959 he lectured at the Sorbonne on the necessary revision of Christian teaching concerning Israel (in the religious, not the political, sense). Two years later The National Conference of Christians and Jews published this lecture under the title "Has Anti-Semitism Roots in Christianity?"—with an introductory essay by Dr. Bernhard Olson, then of Union Theological Seminary, himself a foremost authority on the same subject. Professor Isaac prefaced his lecture with this remark: "In any religious life there are times when an act of purification is called for and cannot be postponed." In his lecture he referred to an eighteen-point program for the reappraisal of Christian education concerning Israel, which he had proposed in 1947. The program included reminding Christians of what their sacred Scriptures really say; how close Jesus was to all of the prophets; and discounting the phrase "The Jews," particularly in the Fourth Gospel, as a collective term for the enemies of Jesus: they actually were a very small proportion of the Jews in Palestine, who in turn were a small proportion of the Jews then living. The program would remind Christians that Jesus never himself ceased to uphold and practice Judaism including the Law, that up to the very end he had enthusiastic sympathy from the Jewish masses, most of whom were not told that he was the Messiah and did not reject him as such. The high priests, says Professor Isaac, were an unrepresentative group "'bound to Rome and detested by the people." The eighteenth point is "And lastly, it should not forget that the monstrous cry: 'His blood be upon us and upon our children' could never prevail against the Word: 'Father, forgive them for they know not what they do.'"

The Council of Trent in the middle of the sixteenth century authorized a catechism which, if widely taught and accepted, would have rendered unnecessary much of the struggle that went on in the Second Vatican Council. In recent years papal action has removed some of the offense from the Catholic liturgy. Conservative elements at the Vatican and in the Council have used various devices to postpone, to modify, and in general to thwart a truly Christian statement by their Church. However, when such a statement, after many vicissitudes and much revision, came before the Council in 1964, it was approved in principle by about eighty-nine percent of the bishops.

Even now that the revised admonitions have become official, generations must still pass before those who accept them succeed in freeing themselves from old and unchristian habits of thought and speech, and still more before their opponents confess that their very arguments and reputed traditions have no real support in the New Testament and are completely alien to the spirit of Jesus. But the responsibility is by no means confined to Catholics, nor are the efforts toward revision. Dr. Olson in *The Christian Advocate* (April 22, 1965) refers to many anti-anti-Semitic statements by other Christians: Anglicans, Lutherans, the National Council of Churches and the World Council of Churches (1961, New Delhi). But for both Protestants and Catholics there remains the work of revising textbooks, changing the attitude of teachers and ministers themselves, and promoting acquaintance with Jewish history and literature, including the Old Testament, and with their Jewish neighbors, not neglecting acquaintance with the Synagogue. This process will involve official and unofficial conversations at denominational and community levels, sometimes between Jews and Protestants, sometimes between Catholics and Jews, sometimes including all three. A Catholic-Jewish Institute was held in January 1965 at Saint Vincent Archabbey, Latrobe, Pennsylvania, with the Project as one of the sponsors. Rabbi Arthur Gilbert, Director of the Project, reports that one of the rabbis wanted to know whether the change in the Church, indicated by discussions in the Second Vatican Council, was genuine. Rabbi Gilbert concluded after four days of dialogue at Latrobe, that such a question need not be raised again: "If anything at all occurred within these four days, it was a growth in trust." We have referred in Chapter 3 to statements by Rabbi Gordis made at the Archabbey.

The author can testify to much conversation and cooperation between the National Council of Churches and Jewish bodies, both religious and secular, from 1951 to 1960, and they are continuing. Reference has already been made to Jewish participation in the National Conference on Religion and Race in 1963: the official participating body was the Synagogue Council of America.

It is perhaps inevitable that as a minority group moves toward full recognition and participation in political life, there will be a phase or a stage of group representation, balanced tickets, and the like. As compared with what may have gone before, the complete ignoring of the given minority, this may be called good, but it is an example of the good which is an obstacle in the way of the best. It tends to crystallize intergroup relations on what can only be accepted, if at all, as a purely temporary basis, and to substitute mere recognition and toleration of differences for the effort at mutual understanding and acceptance, in spite of differences, which is the only possible basis for a peaceful and progressive community.

It is extremely difficult for a Christian to meet his Jewish friends on the basis that each religion is here to stay, deserves the respect of the other, and should not be subjected to the indignity of proselytizing efforts. But any other basis is impossible for the religious Jew. Martin Buber was very positive on this point. The Christian who would like to accept this basis cannot forget the missionary commandment in Holy Scriptures, and it is difficult to see how he could and remain a Christian! He may well remember, however, that Jesus himself said that he came to fulfill, not to destroy; he may well struggle with mind and spirit, earnestly and agonizingly, to distinguish between "witness" and "proselytism." The missionary impulse and duty of the Jew is usually satisfied by the witness of the believer's life, his attitudes and conduct. Surely there can be little doubt that this witness is the essential in any missionary endeavor, a point that was emphasized by Gandhi when asked what Christians must do to improve their missionary effort. But evangelism can, and one would be inclined to say must, employ both the written and the spoken word. This would seem to be legitimate under two conditions. The evangelist must remember that conversion is not his personal triumph: a true conversion can be accomplished only through the action of the Holy Spirit. Evangelism must be approached ecumenically, which means without coercion, overt or covert, with humility and willingness to learn from another faith—in other words in the true spirit of dialogue. And he must remember constantly that his acts and those of others who bear the name of Christian will always speak more emphatically than their words. Let all evangelists try being Christian! An exhortation that ought to be emphasized because it is so frequently violated is implied in the motto of a certain Oxford College, "Manners makyth man." This injunction, often violated by others than evangelists, would forbid any public or private invasion of the sacred precincts of another personality, when there is no explicit or tacit invitation.

In the atmosphere of the growing ecumenical movement Christian and Jewish theologians are approaching each other more and more in the true spirit of dialogue. Christian theologians are abandoning and helping to abolish certain old conceptions, particularly the one that holds that the Jews, having been responsible for the rejection and crucifixion of the Messiah, have been cut off from the Covenant as the chosen people and replaced by Christianity as the true Israel. These theologians are impressed by evidence of continued divine dialogue with the Jewish people, and are asking whether they do not have to deal with two covenants, the continuing one with the Jewish people and the new one in Christianity. In God's plan, of course, the two covenants may well complement each other, and those under each covenant would look and work and pray for a fulfillment which would necessarily include the fulfillment of the other. Conversely, Jewish theologians begin to ponder the significance of the claim of Christianity to be "Israel." Conversations based bilaterally on respect for the convictions which seem to contradict each other fundamentally cannot fail to be fruitful. Rabbi Arthur Gilbert, in *The Lutheran World* of July 1964, wrote:

> Never before in history have Jews and Christians really confronted each other as brothers, each entitled to the dignity of his uniqueness, both respectful of the other's freedom of conscience and right to be. We can at last talk with each other now, in honesty and without fear, because we both sense, somehow, that God will address us through the other. We are attentive and will listen; thus true dialogue is possible.

This means on the one side that Christians are not setting themselves up as judge, jury, and executioner, "trying" the Jews. On the other, it means that Jews must make a superhuman effort to recognize Christian repentance, or even to proceed on the hypothesis that their own readiness to recognize it will help to produce it.

Dialogue even of this high order is only a means to an end. Its working along with other favorable factors will be slow and tedious. Temporal dimensions, in fact, approach the eschatological when one takes into account the necessary growth in grace of

Christians, the absorption and pragmatic inclusion in Christianity of all that Judaism has to contribute to it, and patient waiting for the divine leading. And if, as the temporal merges into the eschatological, we one day find that the Age of the Messiah, which Christians so long put in the past and Jews in the future, has arrived and can be recognized and accepted by both Christians and Jews in the eternal now, we shall surely find that prophecy could not have progressed without the Law, nor the Law without the Prophets.

Dialogue, and such declarations by Christian bodies as we quote below, can only cut the deepest roots of the tree of anti-Semitism and reduce the fertility of the soil which has nurtured it. Meanwhile, the tree remains, and may be fed for a long period from the roots it has in the habits, the traditions, and even in some institutional practices, of our society. This means, among other things, that our civic institutions, our schools, our commerce and our generally humanist culture and all branches of our government have their part to play. What we do and how we behave as individual citizens in every setting is vitally affected by Christian-Jewish relations and is a factor in making them better or worse. We shall, for example, surely discover something important about each other as we work together for better relations between whites and Negroes, as we seek to improve our total educational system, and as we work for peace in our communities and in the world. And as we know each other better, we shall work together more effectively and without lost motion as we seek to make our combined faith more effective in society.

CHRISTIANS OFFICIALLY REPUDIATE ANTI-SEMITISM

All Christians are involved in the heritage of guilt for anti-Semitism, including ancient, recent and current persecution, discrimination and prejudice. They have a common responsibility for making such amends as are possible. It is therefore encouraging to note the declarations of the World Council of Churches, New Delhi, 1961, and the Second Vatican Council, Rome 1965.

Both documents are inadequate as confessions of guilt for the past. It may be that no confession of guilt by churches would be logically or emotionally satisfactory unless undergirded by a sound theological rationale: this was not arrived at by either body. Intra-Christian and Christian-Jewish dialogue will have to wrestle with this.

Both documents are forthright and encouraging as to the removal of abuses in the future. Together, they make it impossible for governments or citizens to believe, assume or pretend that Christianity sanctions any sort of persecution or discrimination against the Jews. Together, they provide the basis for a united and thoroughgoing Christian campaign against anti-Semitism and lay a foundation for improved Christian-Jewish cooperation for human welfare.

Dr. Harvey Cox holds that theology is in the grip of an ecclesiastical bias. He also holds that the first "schism" in the church was that between Christianity and Israel (*The Christian Century*, January 5, 1966). The ecclesiastical declarations of New Delhi and Rome might well become, under the guidance of truly prophetic theologians, Christian and Jewish, a step toward remedying both ills.

8

WORLD PEACE

What do we mean by world peace? Not, for the moment, the road to it, or the need for it, but its necessary and minimum elements. We suggest three. There must be *a tolerable sharing of wealth and power* among the peoples on the globe: if the distribution of either is intolerable, violence between two, or among more, nations ensues. But society is not static: what could be borne yesterday can not be borne today; what we have today we may not be sure of holding tomorrow. There must be *global authorities,* with prescribed principles and procedures, *to redress grievances, correct injustices,* keep the tolerable from becoming intolerable, as long as men are content with justice. But there are nations strong enough or daring enough to commit injustice in the hope of gaining in power or wealth. If "the common sense of most" fails to "hold a fretful realm in awe," the *global authority*—however constituted— must be able *to restrain the aggressor, the rebel, the brigand.* Without the first two elements, the third is impossible or useless. With them, its active intervention would be rarely needed; eventually, its existence and possible exercise would suffice.

The second element is already represented, at least symbolically and potentially, by the World Court. To render it adequate would impose no insuperable obstacles.

The third exists perhaps in embryo in the United Nations. If the first and second elements were substantially realized, the third would present much less difficulty than now confronts us. The United Nations as at present functioning must and can play an

150

important part—through UNICEF, UNESCO, World Health Organization, etc.—in preparing and educating for the first element.

We are not prospecting an easy task, but neither is the concept a visionary one. World peace is no longer an ideal, but a—the—vital and urgent necessity.

We in the United States, in particular, should not shy away from the pursuit and realization of a tolerable distribution, and regulatory and enforcement authorities: we have them. Our distribution is not yet morally tolerable, but it is politically endurable: the nation survives. We criticize the Supreme Court, sometimes bitterly, but both individuals and states eventually obey it—and it in turn, while it may not "follow the elections" in any servile way, eventually bows to the settled convictions of the people. But neither its authority nor the political sovereignty of the central government over the state sovereignties was established without a fratricidal war. But these fifty "sovereign states" have surrendered enough of their claims to permit peace in a vast territory with various interests and cultures. The United States does not constitute, necessarily, a model for world peace, but its history offers encouragement to those willing to look the obstacles in the face.

We meet both similarities and differences as we compare the circumstances in which peace had to be achieved in the United States, beginning two centuries ago, and in the world in our time.

We had and have a large measure of cultural unity in America. In the world, unity of culture is still far off but is favored by instant communications, expanding commerce, and daily increase of intercourse through UNESCO, UNICEF, FAO, WHO, Chambers of Commerce, professional organizations, and the press. As religious bodies become more open to each other and in their attitude to the world, they can accelerate and improve the process of intercultural osmosis and understanding.

The colonies were forced to make and keep the peace with each other in order to be free, strong and prosperous, and the states remain under that necessity. The world, the human race as a whole, must have peace in order not to destroy its civilization, its resources, perhaps its very life: we will avoid war or it will destroy us.

Our thirteen nations surrendered enough sovereignty to purchase some seventy-five years of precarious peace and superficial union; the present fifty, surrendering more, have a more stable peace and a profounder unity. The nations of the world must surrender as much sovereignty, with less assurance of reciprocal trust. Before planes and bombs, we survived a civil war; today, the world must avoid the ambiguities which would lead to such a war, which it can not afford. This we must conclude when we observe the expansion both in magnitude and destructiveness from the American and European wars of the nineteenth century to that of 1914-18 and from that to the 1939-45 World War II—a geometrical ratio in each case.

If the realization of peace is not visionary, neither would the reality be a paradise. We need idealize a world at peace no more than the actuality of the United States at peace. Peace is not an end. It does not assure either human welfare, justice or morality. But it is not only a necessity for survival: it is the condition of further progress toward justice, morality and "the pursuit of happiness."

If world peace is necessary for survival, and a *sine qua non* of man's progress, why have we not achieved it? We have not even set our minds toward it in any focused and concerted fashion. Perhaps—nay, evidently—the focus of needed, purposeful, effective effort has not been clear, and hence is by no means generally recognized. Disarmament, world court, abolition of poverty, conscientious objection, the parliament of man, an order of humanity, and other useful approaches and steps toward peace, or instruments useful in achieving or maintaining peace—all have their dedicated advocates. Most of them are supported by well-directed organizations. But the peace movement presents a chaotic image to the man in the street—if it has attracted his attention.

The author is not insisting that every lover of peace and worker for peace must agree to the three elements he has mentioned and work for their actualization. He is insisting that a broadly-based, highly competent leadership group could and should agree on the minimum essentials of world peace, and begin the work of unifying peace efforts—not by forming one more peace organization, but by persuading leaders and organizations and governments to orient their efforts, however specialized, however general, to realizing the essential ingredients of peace. The essentials must be clearly stated, understandable by all, inclusive of all intelligent and sincere efforts—and adding up to a dynamic peace.

Not everyone sees and feels the possibility or the necessity of peace. "There are worse things than war." Name any two you have in mind: war breeds them, feeds on them. Disease, famine, expatriation, poverty, intolerance, hatred, racism, cruelty, acceptance of evil, fatalism—all thrive on war and breed more war. Some will say that Communism is worse than war: "better dead than red." But it was World War I that permitted Lenin to take over Russia, and World War II opened the way for Mao-tse Tung in China. How many in South Vietnam today would prefer death to the rule of Ho Chi Minh? The people of Russia and Yugoslavia show signs of overcoming the rigidity of Communism. One might with some reason ask whether Fascism is not worse than war. But Fascism *is* war—civil war on its own minorities, and inevitable breeder of international war. Some will point to medical discoveries occasioned or stimulated by war, but one-tenth of one percent of the cost of war, devoted to medical research, could have accomplished more: you don't need tens of millions of guinea-pigs, or millions of fatalities.

Another obstacle in the way of peace is the fatalism of multiplied millions. "You have always had war, you always will." "You can't change human nature!" Yes, but human conduct has been changed time after time, in situation after situation. We do not act in the same way that our forefathers did in every respect. French and Germans have alternated in ravaging each other's territories for centuries, and yet there is evident, especially since World War

II, the possibility of peace, good will, understanding, cooperation between French and Germans.

The evident and awful horror of war, while it has impressed many people, has not proved a sufficient deterrent against war. But people who are not adequately impressed by the loss of human life may be more sensitive, more impressed, if they realize what has actually been the destruction of property. The mute witness of war cemeteries may not be as impressive as great areas, particularly urban, that have been laid waste by war. A moonlight trip from Luxemburg to Verdun after World War I—several years after— showed merely ghosts of towns over a wide devasted and lonely area. After World War II, large parts of London, Bremen, Hamburg, Kassel, Cologne, Frankfurt, Turin, Milan, Cassino were in ruins, a vast, visible, haunting waste—just in the Western nations. (None of that waste, be it noted, was the effect of nuclear bombing.) If the horror of war emphasizes its cruelty, the waste of war emphasizes its sheer stupidity.

After every war, no matter how fairly and justly it may seem to have been settled by the treaty or treaties of peace, there are after-effects of disappointment, of hatred and of desire for revenge, which are fruitful soil for another and later, and perhaps more destructive, war.

There are always those who, for personal or ideological or nationalistic reasons, are ready to exploit these left-overs of hatred and desire for revenge in a way to produce new war, and if there were not enough fruits for this purpose from former wars, there is always enough discontent, pride, ambition, ready for exploitation to tempt both the commercial adventurer and the ideological adventurer. There will be excuses plausible enough for "wars of liberation" until we liberate ourselves from war.

One obvious reason why we do not yet have peace is that we have not brought into being the elements or factors essential to peace. Those mentioned at the beginning of this chapter are not necessarily to be realized in the same order in which they are mentioned. They are, in fact, largely dependent on each other.

Their realization depends not only on overcoming the adverse factors which we have been mentioning but also on the creation of a belief in peace and a will to peace. Here the peace-makers have much to do. Circumstances are converting millions to nuclear pacifism. Nuclear pacifism is somewhat in the same category as the balance of terror and power. That balance is a temporary and precarious protection against war. Similarly, the abolition of nuclear bombs might somewhat diminish the immediate danger of a world holocaust. The same is true of a limited or gradual reduction in arms.

We need, however, to bear in mind at least two considerations. One, to banish a technology and the arms dependent upon it is no guarantee, as long as the knowledge survives, that instruments would not be created if there should be another war. If we began with sticks and stones or bows and arrows, we should proceed inevitably as long as the knowledge is there and the materials for its use, to the use of gun powder, of T.N.T., and of nuclear arms. Even without nuclear arms, one must remember the sort of thing that could be done in Dresden. Here, incendiary bombs were used in sufficient quantity and with sufficient accuracy to produce a fire-storm which fed on itself and consumed a city. In fact, none of the destruction in Europe was produced by nuclear means. We could still commit collective global suicide without either fission or fusion bombs.

Einstein once said that if two percent of the population were conscientious objectors, it would be enough to stop war. There is no evidence that we are likely to have two percent of the population of the world committed to nonviolence and to absolute refusal to serve in war. As long as we are divided into nations with different interests and traditions, we are not likely to have enough trust in the people of a neighbor country or of one across the seas to be willing to risk for our own country the destruction that might follow if we paralyzed our own defense agencies. It is perhaps easier for one to be a conscientious objector in a nation that has strong defenses, natural and military, so that he does not feel that he is taking much risk for himself or for his country by committing himself not to bear arms. The motivation for conscientious objection may also be reduced by the feeling that one's country has been deprived, through colonialism or other exploitation or through past wars, of its just opportunities and its proper share in the world's wealth and power. There are many who believe with all their soul and mind and heart that war is wrong, but they have not the courage of their convictions.

Much more could be said concerning obstacles to peace in general and what religious forces can and should do to overcome or remove them, but we pass first to some obstacles in the way of a tolerable distribution of wealth and power. C. P. Snow, echoing Lincoln, has said that the world cannot survive half rich and half poor.

Almost everywhere in the world there are legacies of colonialism, imperialism and other forms of exploiting minorities. We proudly and with unclouded conscience disclaim any desire for conquest—having pushed the aborigines around in the continental United States, Hawaii and Alaska, overpowered Mexico in a war not wholly defensive, and engaged no little in dollar diplomacy and economic imperialism. We are in no moral position to curb the greed of the powerful or quiet the fears of the poor and weak.

We are a charitable people, but charity is not enough—nor are we charitable *enough*. What is needed is not the sharing of our abundance—except temporarily, to meet an emergency. America and all the rich and powerful industrial nations must share their experience and their technology with the nations still in the pre-industrial stage. If they are enabled to help themselves, and if access to markets is kept open on an equitable basis, the whole world can be immeasurably enriched. If the whole approach and effort is not international—well-nigh universal—there must at least be some ground rules and some division of labor, taking account of the varying and special skills and resources of the helping countries.

And here one encounters the population problem: the fact that production and consumption have never existed in a tolerable ratio. The ratio is worse than it need be, because of poor distribution. It is also likely to be worse for a time as the standard of living, the level of consumption, rises in the poorer areas. For population is likely to increase even faster, with more food and better health. As a people rises from bare subsistence to a moderate level of comfort, families begin to be concerned for education and suitable employment, and the birth rate moves toward correspondence with the opportunity in prospect for the child.

The natural increase of the earth's population has until now been limited by disease, famine and war. All are economically disastrous and morally intolerable. "Birth control" is a crude and repulsive idea when it implies external interference, especially governmental, in the rights and responsibilities of parents. "Responsible parenthood" puts the onus where it belongs. But as a means of population control it is a long way off. It need not divide Protestants and Catholics if each is willing and able to understand and respect the other's conscience.

A policy question of considerable gravity is whether and to what extent the government of the United States or the United Nations can promote the use of contraceptive devices among people who have no conscientious objection to their use. Foreign aid, governmental or voluntary, including health measures, while morally and politically imperative, is dependent on the support of persons who are critical, easily discouraged—many seeking grounds of discouragement! If a glaring consequence of assistance is a net increase in hungry mouths, is there not danger that both self-interest and generosity will give way to apathy, perplexity, and a disposition to let the rest of the world minister to its own ills? This is not to imply that if contraceptives were freely accessible the population problem would be solved, or that moral convictions should be overridden in favor of a doubtful panacea. Each reader is invited to consider the policy question of this paragraph with a seriousness that matches the gravity of the question.

Much more can be done and must be done to increase food

production and distribute it better. In the name of what divinity or moral principle do we pay farmers not to produce when not only our "enemies" but our friends are dying of hunger? There are many friends of peace and justice who believe that there is really no population problem, but only the problem, the task, of increased production and better distribution. It is a sobering thought that there has never been enough food available to prevent diseases of malnutrition, starvation, famine: we do not start from scratch. Furthermore, with our present efforts we are not gaining but losing ground: the world production of food increased in 1965 by roughly one percent; population, approximately two percent (*The New York Times*, January 4, 1966).

The population pressure is not only on food supply: people must have education, employment, leisure, water, living space and accommodations (eventually, standing room and breathable air!).

Only a concerted effort by all the earth's peoples can achieve and maintain a tolerable ratio between the earth's available material resources and the number of the world's inhabitants. Unilateral aid and bilateral cooperation are useful, commendable steps, but the task is too big and too long for an uncoordinated effort. As the newly awakened peoples strive for stability and prosperity, revolutions are inevitable. But they would not all play into the hands of Communist powers as so-called "wars of liberation" if those powers could be involved in a cooperative—at least a coordinated—approach for the worldwide abolition of poverty. An invitation from the United Nations to join in the effort, if backed by the assured participation of the non-Communist powers, would expose any insincerity in their ideologically oriented efforts to liberate an area and a people from "capitalist imperialism." It might well persuade some European Communist nations that aid is cheaper and more effective than military intervention. Most nations, if not all, stand in need of the same persuasion.

It is evident that confidence in an established means for maintaining a just distribution would greatly aid in bringing about such distribution. Injustices and grievances must be dealt with as they arise—inevitably—during the very process of seeking to bring about a less unjust distribution of the world's resources and opportunities. Conversely, as the underprivileged, underpropertied peoples became convinced of the sincerity and justice of the global effort, their confidence in the World Court or equivalent would increase. The United States can not very effectively urge trust in the World Court until it at least repeals the Connally proviso and shows its readiness to submit to the Court any question that involves our relations with another nation. Neither pride, conscious power nor a provincial and anachronistic isolationism should restrain us. It should be our pride to demonstrate our trust in a court that embodies the pick of the world's judges and the distillation of its judicial experience and principles.

But we come to the heart of our problem when we ask how decisions of the World Court or of the United Nations (or equivalent global authorities) are to be enforced on the recalcitrant.

National spirit has been a major factor in developing national character and, in the fields of commerce and of culture, has been of great value to mankind as a whole, through competition as well as cooperation. With most of the nations of the world still in the first hundred and fifty years of their independence, and with perhaps half of the young nations of Asia and Africa in their first quarter-century, there might be great loss if national spirit by some miracle were suddenly and fully submerged in the international spirit. Yet the national spirit must learn to yield to international necessities, just as the fifty states of our Union must go on learning to limit their fancifully labeled "sovereignty," and their very genuine states' rights, to the requirements of the nation and the people as a whole. It will take a long time for both the new nations and the old to learn that sovereignty for them is also largely a fetish, not an unlimited existential fact. National spirit is too often an undisciplined nationalism, assuming to ride roughshod over the rights, and in spite of the national spirit, of its neighbors.

The kind of world order in which peace might be possible on the basis of enforceable international agreements has long been an ideal. Now it has become a necessity. Nationalism must be curbed without damage to national spirit. The seal and symbol of this necessity are the atom and hydrogen bombs.

But nationalism, national spirit unrestrained, is not going to yield to exhortation, or even to demonstrable necessity, without pressures of other kinds. It is a way of life, an ingrained habit, for the nations and for most of their citizens. The nation is the only real divinity, sanctifying not only what is right, but wholesale murder and devastation as the occasion demands: "my country, right or wrong." He who protests is not only regarded as a traitor but as some sort of infidel. If he undertakes to speak and act in the name of humanity, he is at best an impractical and deluded visionary. Since Communists often use the word peace, its use by others easily gives rise to the epithet, "red." This situation is a source of power for organizations and individuals of the right, extreme and not so extreme.

Fear of Communism—real and serious—in defeated Germany and disappointed Italy was adroitly, almost magically, woven into a fanatical nationalism that produced tyranny at home, a global holocaust, its own defeat—and a much vaster and mightier world Communism. Fascism and nationalism are Siamese twins, ideologically kin. While Communism can use nationalism and has used it effectively, nationalism has also divided world Communism. The only point of this paragraph is that Fascism is a dangerous agent to employ against Communism. Better stick to democracy—as fast as we can achieve it in spite of racism, anti-Semitism, the intrenched powers of capital and labor, and the inertia of a too complacent citizenry.

Diplomacy is still almost entirely based on nationalist premises, habits and traditions. While the United Nations offers an opportunity to change the assumptions and develop new approaches, Adlai Stevenson's hands were tied by the old. Diplomacy is still, in general, not directed toward peace, but toward securing national advantage by peace or war, regarding war and diplomacy as a continuum, according to the Clausewitz dictum.

Psychologically, we are in a dilemma. We will not forsake our nationalist habits until we have a world authority that commands our confidence; a world authority cannot be strong enough to command our confidence until we forsake our nationalism! Actually, each process is a gradual one, and international processes may be gradually substituted for unilateral ones. But the substitution will not develop, or be made rapidly enough, unless we make up our minds as to which way we want to go.

And here the religious bodies have an imperative duty and a great opportunity. The conciliar bodies—Vatican Council, World and National Councils of Churches—are committed in principle and by many acts and public statements to the support of a world organization for peace with justice. In the United Nations, secular forces will seem to some to have advanced much further than religious forces. One must take account, however, of the large part played directly and indirectly by religion and religious leaders in creating the demand for the U.N., in the drafting of the Charter, in continuing criticism and counsel through resident observers, and through the support of the World Council of Churches and the Vatican. The World Council's Commission of the Churches on International Affairs with an able staff and directing membership does valuable research and policy studies and publicizes its views and recommendations with effective aid from the press. The Second Vatican Council effectively related the abolition of poverty to world peace. More eloquent and moving was Pope John's *Pacem in Terris*. More spectacular and more daring was Pope Paul's appearance before the United Nations.

Both the Catholic Church and the World Council (Protestant and Eastern Orthodox) are world bodies. But their constituencies are by no means free from nationalism. They and the various non-Christian religious leaders have a long road ahead to educate and convert their followers to a determined will to peace.

A promising effort in that direction was the National Inter-Religious Peace Conference in Washington, D.C., in March 1966. It may well take its place in the ecumenical impact alongside the similar conference on race relations in Chicago three years earlier. There is prospect of cooperation with the confessional "umbrella" bodies which, however, did not officially sponsor the peace conference as they did the one on race.

There is also a plan to extend the Washington movement to other religions and other nations. While this might dilute the theological content, it should facilitate two of the principal tasks of the peace forces. The wish for peace must be converted into the determined will to peace, and this requires the sober conviction that a tolerable peace is possible. And among every people there must be acceptance of a patriotism that includes all humanity in its *patria,* and commitment to work for the essentials of world peace: a long road—and a short time.

9

CONSENSUS, DIALOGUE, AND THE ECUMENICAL IMPACT

Following two chapters in which the general relations of religion with society, especially its political and economic aspects, were briefly reviewed, we have been considering—also briefly—several areas of great, even desperate, social concern where vital questions remain in controversy, sometimes healthy, sometimes frustrating.

These involve church-state relations, religion and education, law and morality, racial and religio-ethnic minorities and the struggle against poverty and war.

How much agreement is indispensable for the welfare, even the existence, of the social order? By what means shall we seek necessary and beneficial consensus? What is religion's role in the search?

A prior question for the religious forces is how they are to achieve enough agreement and cooperation among themselves to contribute to necessary social harmony. That question has been frequently explicit in every chapter. Fortunately, the priority of the problem does not demand a complete priority of solution: even a faltering step in the right direction makes the next step easier.

How much consensus is necessary for a viable society? How much is needed for a great society? We have seen that in the United States there is not yet enough consensus in some matters with regard to producing and sustaining a society that is either good or great. This is true with regard to the acceptance of Negroes—in housing, jobs, schools, human relations, politics, or churches. It is true with regard to the causes and cure of poverty, to a bad food-population ratio. It is true with regard to the clashes of nations and of ideologies.

If not consensus, at least pragmatic assent or passive acquiescence is required at some points if we are to have anything that can be called a society or a nation—anything, that is, but anarchy. Interestingly enough, anarchy in its etymological sense, the absence of government, is consistent only with complete consensus on all vital points. We seem to have in the United States at least a tacit working agreement—workable after a fashion—that we wish to remain one nation with majority rule under law, consistent with the Federal Constitution. We submit to measures that the majority considers necessary for national independence and self-defense, for a minimum of some sort of education, for some regulation of traffic, and for some protection against disease and crime. Most of us believe that our system is the best yet devised for such a people as we are, and that it provides such excellent means for its own improvement that we don't think at all of changing to another system.

It is possible for the apparent consensus to be excessive. This happens, for example, under the coerced conformity of a dictatorship. But a deadening conformity has also come about at some times and places through acceptance of the *status quo,* complacent on the part of the rich and powerful, fatalistic on the part of the poor and weak.

In an imperfect and constantly changing society, changing because of world advances in science and world cultural evolution, pluralism offers an advantageous alternative both to a coerced and to a complacent conformity. Pluralism is not so much a good to be sought or praised as an existing condition from which we may and must profit. An inevitable result of differences that have remote but persistent historical, religious, economic and ethnic origins, a tolerated pluralism can stimulate the various vocal (and voting) groups in our economy both to compete and to cooperate in the search for improvement, provided they maintain communication with each other.

There seems to be a large measure of consensus in the United States on several vital points. One is the division of responsibility and authority with regard to local, state and national government. There are points where the national must prevail, and here there is not perhaps as yet adequate consensus. There is still a fallacious affirmation of state sovereignty, which was valid under the articles of confederation, which survived long enough to provoke a fratricidal war a century ago and which still bedevils necessary and proper discussion of the best division of responsibility. This fallacy in recent years, one can almost say from the beginning of federal government, has been used to bolster white supremacy. Serious problems have arisen and interesting experiments are beginning with dimensions that do not fit neatly into this threefold classification. Some are interstate or regional, as for example the water problem in the Southwest and in the Northeast. Some are metropolitan, such as the tax question and the traffic problem of Greater New York. Although an adequate consensus does not yet exist, at least there is growing agreement that the problems exist and must be solved.

There also seems to be, since the shock of our failure to join the League of Nations, an increasing conviction that we cannot withdraw from the world. But isolationism is by no means dead. With a combination of deadly fear and chauvinistic self-assurance we are always in danger of burying our heads in the selfish and deceptive security of "fortress America." The measure of consensus with regard to our role in the world is closely related to the development of an international consensus. There are many who refuse to put any confidence or trust in co-existence with the nations of Eastern Europe, and see no hope of our survival and that of the West unless we inflict a military defeat on the still more intransigent governments beyond the "bamboo curtain." The near hysteria and fanaticism of that position is partly counterbalanced by a growing conviction that nothing we hold dear (including ourselves!) would survive a nuclear holocaust.

In the field of education there seems to be wider agreement as to the need for education and as to a very inclusive responsibility for it than as to content and method. With regard to responsibility, however, we vary greatly as to just how it is to be shared by parents, government, and churches in the total community, and by local, state and federal authorities.

There are probably few Americans today who would deny some doctrine of church-state separation. But the meaning, manner and degree and the fundamental reasons for it vary in kaleidoscopic fashion.

The incompatibility of racism and democracy seems to be increasingly admitted. But many who practice or acquiesce in one form of racism or another find their own definitions for racism and democracy in order to excuse themselves: a glaring example is afforded by the difficulty of securing legislation and compliance with it for open-occupancy housing.

Perhaps a link which connects all of the areas where we have been seeking consensus is to be found in the greater or lesser emphasis attached to individualism. Surely it is a part of our American heritage to emphasize the value and the freedom of the individual. But some of us err grievously by exaggerating our own individual rights. We hesitate to accept any doctrine of collective rights for fear of promoting socialism—toward some variety of which every government on earth is moving, not because of theory or doctrine, but in an effort to meet recognized needs of society as a whole. Far more reasonable is the fear of Communism. But if we are unable to distinguish between any variety of socialism and an aggressive, materialistic, atheistic, nationalistic Communism, we do not have the wisdom required, not only for co-existence, but for existence in today's world. It is also of urgent importance that we examine and evaluate those changes in world conditions in the international equilibrium and within the societies of Eastern Europe which justify continued experiments in the direction of coexistence. A national commission of economists, statesmen, scientists, educators, and churchmen, supported by a foundation or by the government, should undertake this task without further loss of time.

The amount and nature of the American consensus on several points seems to be dangerously inadequate. Perhaps the most immediately dangerous inadequacy is our lack of agreement as to how we should deal with Communism and Communists, domestic and foreign. Closely related is our hesitancy as to the value and function of the United Nations and our in-and-out reliance upon it and cooperation with it as troubles arise in various parts of the world.

By no means remote from the problems just mentioned are questions relating to freedom of speech, publication, assembly and demonstration—all guaranteed within necessary limits by the Constitution.

These questions in turn are intimately bound up with our understanding of majority rule. The necessary prevalence of the majority when a choice becomes imperative in order that government may proceed gives no moral right or political wisdom to the roughshod overriding of minorities. Their rights are as important as those of the majority. Not infrequently their wisdom is of superior quality. In case after case, if minority voices were taken into account, better solutions would be reached than those proposed and imposed by the majority.

With regard to the relation between morality and law, although it would be difficult to estimate the seriousness of the variations in our attitudes, it can scarcely be assumed that we have reached an adequate consensus. Questions arise with regard to three areas. In sex morality we are not agreed as to the danger to society of promiscuity—premarital or other—divorce, contraception, the treatment of homosexuals. With regard to criminals we are far from agreed as to the respective roles of punishment and reformation. The parole system and the conditions for the release of patients from mental hospitals are neither adequate nor uniform. Unless there is careful examination before release, based on something more than leniency or need for the quarters they occupy, and adequate counselling and supervision after release, the process is a very risky one. Who should censor publications, plays and broadcasts, on what grounds, and when, are questions that receive the most varied and confusing answers. How to protect the young and innocent, not only from invitations to immorality but from deformation of taste, would perplex the best-intentioned and the most law-abiding. Between anarchy and tyranny the range is wide, and the dangers in either direction are formidable.

As perhaps this whole book has illustrated, we are far from agreement either as to the function of religion in society or as to the necessary content of any religion whose existence and impact upon society might be deemed essential. What are the limits of toleration? Who is to determine them, if any limits are necessary? How far may the forces of religion and of government cooperate with benefit to both and therefore to society? How far can the nation rely upon science and humanism and ignore the actual and potential contributions of religion? Are there vital problems for men and nations for which science alone cannot provide solutions?

Before proceeding to the question of how we should seek consensus, let us note the danger in one kind of consensus, that based on the leader. The Western world by this time ought to be sufficiently aware of the totalitarian danger illustrated by Mussolini, Hitler, Stalin. We are less sensitive to the dangers of benevolent dictatorships, if we dare to apply the term to Franco, Salazar, or Tito. Most of us are still less aware of what persons close to them noted or thought they saw of Franklin Roosevelt and of Pius XII. As their days in office were prolonged year after year there is some evidence that it became increasingly difficult for each of them to remember that he might make a mistake. The broader, the more nearly universal is the support for a leader, the more likely even a great leader is to take for granted that the voice of the people is indeed the voice of God.

THE NATURE AND THE FUNCTION OF
DIALOGUE

Very little has been attempted by way of answering the questions or suggesting solutions to the problems outlined so far in this chapter. An answer or a solution sociologically and politically viable is much more likely to be arrived at by a process involving the various interests in a given community or in the nation than by the advocacy of this or that solution. The advocacy of one's own views is both necessary and proper within that process, but at this point we should look at the process, which we may call dialogue.

The term "dialogue" has been so much before our eyes and in our ears in recent years that many persons tend to dismiss the whole idea as being already passé. The contrary, almost the opposite, is true. We are only at the beginning of dialogue and of the exploration and determination of its usefulness—let alone its exhaustion—in society.

A lesser danger is that dialogue be sought, promoted, experienced as an end in itself. This came very near to being the case a generation ago with "discussion groups." The effectiveness of the discussion group as a technique, depending as it did to a large degree on the skill of its leader, came in many instances to overshadow its usefulness as an intellectual stimulus or a sociological instrument. The dialogue that we are considering depends much less on any individual, much more on the purpose, concern and participation of the given group as a whole. By dialogue we intend sincere speaking and earnest listening in the discussion of matters of common concern with regard to which important differences exist in the given group or community.

Dialogue is to be distinguished from unilateral propaganda, from open debate, and from the forum. Opinions and interests may be in such sharp conflict that vigorous debate of a partisan and polemical character is required in order to locate and define the contested issues and to clarify them sufficiently that the more tentative, more friendly and more hopeful process of dialogue may be usefully employed. Perhaps the difference between the two processes may be made clearer if we say that the normal result of debate is a majority vote for the side that may really have the better of the argument or may, on the other hand, merely have the most plausible and persuasive argument and debating style. While debate permits, or may permit, the minority to be heard, it frequently falls far behind dialogue in assuring that minority opinions and interests are given the adequate, the necessary, consideration. Dialogue tends not toward the victory of one party or one opinion, but to an agreement that approaches unanimity where unanimity is conceivable, and mutual understanding where all concerned recognize that there are some differences which are not in the given situation reconcilable. While discussion in a decision-making body of Friends may be far from verbose, it is true dialogue because it assumes the need and the possibility of arriving at a solution or an interim decision which all can accept. No one is overpowered; no one expresses assent until he feels that he has adequately expressed his dissent, that it has been given reasonable consideration, and that even if he is not fully persuaded, he is ready to trust the wisdom of the group as a whole. Obviously there are few groups in society characterized by the unanimity of spirit, of experience, and of purpose which characterizes the Quakers. But also there are few groups that could not profit from the example which they set. It is also true that there are many religious bodies, theoretically as fully unilateral in doctrine and in spirit as the Friends, which still cling to debate and majority vote in arriving at decisions of momentous concern to those who may be outvoted and to the body as a whole.

Long experience with the ecumenical movement among Christian individuals and bodies tends to support the judgment that historically and in its present development it is essentially dialogue. As long as, and in so far as, there is not that acquaintance and mutual trust among at least a few significant leaders in Christian denominations or confessions, the ecumenical movement cannot begin, or its progress is blocked. This necessary acquaintance was being developed through several decades among theologians, Protestant, Catholic and Orthodox, who read each other's writings, were sometimes members of the same theological faculty, and discussed unofficially the similarities and differences of their discoveries.

Added to the influence of theologians was a growing conviction in the churches, to which many theologians contributed, that the churches' mission cannot be fully understood or effectively carried on if the churches remain in the attitude of defensive, self-oriented institutionalism.

There has been, also, a growing realization that the unity of all Christians will increase the evangelical and social impact. This does not necessarily mean one big church or even the administrative coordination of all Christian churches. It seems more probable that union, when it comes, will come as a result of unity, than that we should seek union regardless of differences in the hope that it will bring unity. We are so far, at present, from either that we need not take time in the present context to examine arguments for supporting one process or the other. There is enough desire and conviction in support of both unity and union to make the continuing dialogue imperative. Both the Vatican and the World Council of Churches have recognized this fact, and have begun serious dialogue of an official but as yet exploratory character. One of their subjects for discussion is dialogue!

One of the areas where true dialogue has been most needed and most lacking has been that of race relations. For many generations communication has been between the white "big I" and the Negro "little you." Between the two World Wars there were small and significant beginnings of real dialogue, backed by a few church leaders and by the Student Christian Associations. These beginnings could not be stigmatized as too late so far as those involved were concerned, but they were certainly too little so far as the churches and society were concerned. They were an example of real communication and constructive dialogue, but they had not gone far in replacing the old style of communication between the inheritors and the disinherited. They had not even sufficed to warn the power structure that a new pattern of communication was imperative and inevitable if the social fabric was not to disintegrate. The Supreme Court decision of 1954 helped to awake the white leaders. But it also aroused a frenzy of desperation among ignorant and reactionary whites, many of whom were as disinherited, culturally and economically speaking, as their Negro neighbors, but were ignorant of their poverty because they gloried in their white skin and borrowed superiority. The experience of the small groups that engaged in dialogue before World War II provides ample encouragement to those who would restore communication along horizontal lines rather than lines slanting downward. Additional encouragement and evidence are afforded by the experience of an institute or workshop which met at the University of Oklahoma in May 1965. There, white and Negro leaders, mainly from the South, discussed the most controversial questions in race relations in an atmosphere and a spirit of genuine dialogue. Obviously the experience of such conversations should be widespread, repeated in one city and one university after another, not only across the South but throughout the nation. It is by no means certain that interracial dialogue, though no less needed, would be any more easy or effective in other parts of the nation than in the South.

The National Conference of Christians and Jews, while claiming and enjoying no monopoly or even priority in the field of dialogue, seems to be the only organization seeking to promote, aid and coordinate dialogue on a national scale. Its efforts in this field have been greatly stimulated since 1961 through its Project on Religious Freedom and Public Affairs. As of May 1965, there were eighty-seven dialogue groups in fifty-nine communities involving laymen as well as clergy. These were usually stimulated or instituted by local or national representatives of the NCCJ. They were aided by a number of institutes dealing with different topics. They also had the use of some thirty issues of *Dialogue,* a bulletin, dealing with more than a dozen topics. The Director of the Project, Rabbi Arthur Gilbert, in summarizing his conclusions as the cycle terminated, made several interesting observations. The nature of the controversy in each religious community was at last becoming more sophisticated: "We were no longer tilting at the windmills of caricature—rather we confronted each other with masks removed and faced the real issues." Dr. Philip Scharper, in addressing the NCCJ staff in October 1964, had also referred to the Protestant mask fashioned by Catholics and Jews; the Jewish mask, by Protestants and Catholics; and the Catholic mask, by Jews and Protestants. Dr. Scharper underscored the role which the NCCJ must play in the area of race relations, calling on it "to strengthen the spiritual consensus which for the religiously committed is required for compliance." He spoke with equal significance of the role of dialogue concerning public education, parochial schools, theology, Christian-Jewish relations, and in general recognizing the relevance of religion to the temporal order.

Rabbi Gilbert in his report also pointed out that we differ with each other not only on religious grounds but as citizens. Interreligious dialogue can help us reach a common understanding of the meaning of religious freedom, the intent of the First Amendment, and the proper exercise of authority by the legislature or the Supreme Court, and the resolution of social conflict. "Finally," Rabbi Gilbert observed, "the success of the dialogue program in the handling of interreligious conflict has suggested to many that it can be an effective device for dealing with other problems in the public order. . . . It has now been utilized for conversations between clergy and police; clergy, labor and business officials; clergy and civil rights organizations." In many communities, he reported, the dialogue groups have led to more formal and official structure for interreligious conversations or cooperative social action.

Local Councils of Churches are usually the result of dialogue, and dialogue is a large part of their effective technique. It is probably the atmosphere and spirit which have brought about Roman Catholic participation in a few places on the part of a congregation or a diocese. Pope John and Vatican II have favored and demonstrated the spirit and method of dialogue, so that their participation in a Council of Churches with Protestants, Anglicans and Eastern Orthodox is far easier and more natural than it would have been even as late as 1958.

CAN RELIGION DO A BETTER JOB?

Little reflection, little review of history, little pondering of what has been written in this book, is required to support the conviction and the conclusion that religious forces, and particularly the Christian churches, have frequently "left undone those things which they ought to have done and done those things which they ought not to have done." The same is true of individuals. Obviously the institutions and the individuals could find enough stimulus in their own doctrine and conscience to remedy many of their shortcomings and to exercise a more profound and beneficent influence, both on individuals and on society, than they have done in the past. Much of the needed stimulus is to be found in the good, great, and holy deeds of the past. But it becomes increasingly evident that united we stand, divided we continue to stumble, occasionally fall, and in general come far short of our high calling.

United we stand, and can overcome. There is less wasted energy, there is better use of laymen, there is the stimulus of friends instead of the self-serving denunciation by the self-righteous. Christians must accept the prayer of Jesus in John XXI as evidence that if his followers are united the world is more likely to believe in him.

It should be abundantly clear that Christians bear no monopoly of responsibility either for the failures or the successes of religion in the world. However, the ecumenical movement is a little further along internally among Christians than it is between Christians and Jews; still more than it is between Christians and Mohammedans or the non-theistic religions. The major emphasis in our consideration of the increased impact of religion on society because of the ecumenical movement will therefore be on the Christian ecumenical movement. Part of that impact involves the influence of the Christian ecumenical movement on other religions, and the resulting increased sensitivity of Christianity to them, their needs, and their contributions.

Some Christians in full allegiance to the ecumenical movement, and more who entertain both organizational and doctrinal scepticism with regard to it, point out one danger which should not be overlooked. It is probably true that many of the shortcomings of the pre-Reformation Church in the Western world were due to its monolithic structure, to an authority that was not questioned internally or externally, and to a resulting complacency. In so far as the new ecumenical movement should fall into the hands of a group of the elite, master minds and master spirits, there would be the grave danger of a new and bigger "establishment." Some denominations, quite apart from ecumenism, have abundantly illustrated the dangers we have in mind. They could invade the ecumenical movement itself. The demon of establishment merits resistance by fasting and prayer.

It would be hazardous to say that religion has failed society more than education, government, business, or even science. Marvelous as the successes of science have been, they are morally colorless. While they diminish our ignorance, they increase our capacity for evil as well as for good. But it is no proper defense of religion to suggest that it has not failed more than other forces in improving society: its aims and standards and claims must be of a higher order. What religion has to add is not only a fundamental and essential aspect of truth; it must add faith, without which mountains of immorality, injustice, selfishness, complacency and indifference cannot be moved.

Among the successes of religion in its service to society, at least relative and partial, we may note its civilizing, humanizing, restraining influence, and the salvage wrought by its compassion.

Among its wrongdoings, shortcomings and at least partial and temporary failures we must note religious wars and hatred, and anti-Semitism. We cannot dismiss also the frequent fear and scepticism of religion with regard to truths established by science and hence with regard to science and scientific method. There have also been centuries of emphasizing a faith focused on the next life, with the resulting neglect of this life and the world in which it is lived. To that degree religion, and particularly Christianity, has often been to a large extent truly the opium of the people. On the part of all religions there has been usually acquiescence in national or regional culture and policy, including the acceptance of internal and external injustices such as slavery, colonialism, the exploitation of labor, the sanctification of property and property rights, dynastic and imperialistic wars. Small wonder, therefore, that Christian missions, in spite of their divine sanction, have frequently been attended with mixed results because of their all-too-human agents and agencies.

However strong a case could be made as to the past and present value of religion to society—and it is a strong one—that is not the focus of this book. The value can be immensely increased! Religion and religious institutions must constantly be purified, reformed, renewed: the Second Vatican Council is eloquent witness as to what must be done, what can be done, and how difficult it is. But more is needed.

In problem after problem, controversy after controversy, we have found the challenge for all men of faith to coordinate their search for true insights and promising solutions, and to unite their efforts. So united, they will be able to enlist also the secularists who share their concern and their aims—or give effective support if secularists have already taken the lead. Surely we do not need further convincing that religion has and needs no monopoly of social concern. Its concern for the individual goes deeper and higher than that of the humanist (who of course denies that there *is* a deeper and higher concern than his). The only interest of society in religion is the question whether religion's transcendent values can be made to validate and reinforce the immanent values that society recognizes and seeks.

Religion's primary social role, therefore, is not to popularize itself, to join the most promising secular movement. It may properly do both, but only as it can agree with the concern and the goal on the basis of its own faith. It can do so effectively if it helps to deepen the general concern, and add dedicated and undiscourageable supporters and leaders to the movement.

Religion therefore, if it is to add a plus to movements for social betterment, must not abandon its evangelism. The "birth control" that is most needed is to multiply the number of Harold Begbie's "twice-born" men. They must be born anew not only to a transcendent faith, but to a new, deeper concern for their fellow men. A great society is not possible, or desirable, unless it is a good society, where every member sees and seeks his own good in terms of every man's good. But enlightened self-interest (true religion does enlighten) is not enough.

We began, nine chapters back, with a reference to the intersection of man's horizontal and vertical relationships. Prophets, martyrs, and many more ordinary mortals have come to the intersection and found that there a cross is hung. The price of one's own integrity—be he Christian or Jew, theist or atheist, pragmatist or mystic—is to sacrifice his own temporal good for the general and lasting good. Without payment of that price on the part of a few, and willingness on the part of many to pay it, the great society (if it does not become a nightmare) must remain a dream.

A SELECT BIBLIOGRAPHY

Berger, Peter L. *The Noise of the Solemn Assemblies: Christian Commitment and the Religious Establishment in America.* Garden City: Doubleday, 1961.

Brown, Robert M., and Weigel, Gustave, S.J. *An American Dialogue. A Protestant Looks at Catholicism and a Catholic Looks at Protestantism.* Garden City: Doubleday Anchor Book, 1960.

Callahan, Daniel J., Oberman, Heiko A., and O'Hanlon, Daniel J., S.J., eds. *Christianity Divided.* New York: Sheed & Ward, 1961.

Campbell, Will D. *Race and the Renewal of the Church.* Philadelphia: The Westminster Press, 1962.

Cate, William B. *Ecumenical Scandal on Main Street.* New York: Association Press, 1965.

Cépede, M., Houtart, F., and Grond, L. *Population and Food.* New York: Sheed and Ward, 1964.

Christman, Henry M., ed. *Peace and Arms: Reports from the Nation.* New York: Sheed & Ward, 1963.

Conant, James B. *Slums and Suburbs.* New York: The New American Library of World Literature, Inc. A Signet Book. 1961.

Cox, Harvey. *The Secular City: Secularization and Urbanization in the Theological Perspective.* New York: The Macmillan Company, 1965.

Daniel, Bradford, ed., *Black, White and Gray.* New York: Sheed & Ward, 1963.

Dialogue. Second Vatican Council Numbers. New York: National Council of Christians and Jews. (Third and Fourth Sessions available)

Documents of Vatican II, The. New York: The America Press, 1966.

Duff, Edward. *The Social Thought of the World Council of Churches.* New York: Association Press, 1956.

Dunne, George H., ed. *Poverty in Plenty.* New York: P. J. Kenedy & Sons, 1964.

Egan, Eileen. *The Works of Peace.* New York: Sheed & Ward, 1966.

Gibbs, James E., and others. *Dual Enrollment: In Public and Non-Public Schools.* Washington, D.C.: United States Department of Health and Welfare, Office of Education, 1965.

Gilbert, Rabbi Arthur. *A Jew in Christian America.* New York: Sheed & Ward, 1966.

Grier, George and Eunice. *Equality and Beyond: Housing Segregation and the Goals of the Great Society.* New York: Anti-Defamation League.

Harrington, Michael. *The Other America.* New York: The Macmillan Company, 1962.

Isaac, Jules. *Has Anti-Semitism Roots in Christianity?* (Introductory essay by Bernard Olson). New York: National Conference of Christians and Jews. (a brochure)

John XXIII, Pope. *Mater et Magistra, Christianity and Social Progress.* New York: The America Press, 1961.

Keith-Lucas, Alan. *The Church and Social Welfare.* Philadelphia: The Westminster Press, 1962.

Kitagawa, Daisuke. *The Pastor and the Race Issue.* New York: Seabury Press, 1965.

Lenski, Gerhard. *The Religious Factor, A Sociological Study of Religion's Impact on Politics, Economics, and Family Life.* Rev. ed. Garden City: Doubleday Anchor Book, 1963.

Murray, John Courtney. *The Problem of Religious Freedom.* Westminster: The Newman Press, 1965.

New Delhi Report, The, ed. W. A. Visser't Hooft. New York: Association Press, 1963.

Nielsen, Niels C., Jr. *God in Education: A New Opportunity for American Schools.* New York: Sheed & Ward, 1966.

Parkes, James. *Anti-Semitism: A Concise World History.* Chicago: Quadrangle Books, 1963.

Pelikan, Jaroslav. *The Riddle of Roman Catholicism.* Memphis: Abingdon, 1959.

President's Committee on Youth Employment. *The Challenge of Jobless Youth.* Washington: United States Department of Labor, 1963.

Scharper, Philip, ed. *Torah and Gospel: Jewish and Catholic Theology in Dialogue.* New York: Sheed & Ward, 1966.

Shinn, Roger L. *Tangled World.* New York: Charles Scribner's Sons, 1965.

Spike, Robert W. *The Freedom Revolution and the Churches.* New York: Association Press, 1965.

Tillman, James A. *Not By Prayer Alone.* A report on the Greater Minneapolis Interfaith Fair Housing Program. Philadelphia: United Church Press, 1964.

Warren, Robert Penn. *Who Speaks for the Negro?* New York: Random House, 1965.

Washington, Joseph R., Jr. *Black Religion, The Negro and Christianity in the United States.* Boston: Beacon Press, 1964.

Weaver, Robert. *The Urban Complex: Human Values and Urban Life.* Garden City: Doubleday Anchor Book, 1964.

Winter, Gibson. *The New Creation as Metropolis.* New York: The Macmillan Company, 1963.